back
roads

back roads

Ted

Ferguson

NeWest Press

C

Library and Archives Canada Cataloguing in Publication

Ferguson, Ted
Back roads / Ted Ferguson.

ISBN 978-1-897126-21-9

1. Ferguson, Ted. 2. Country life--Alberta, Northern. 3. Authors,
Canadian (English)--20th century--Biography. 4. Alberta,
Northern--Biography. I. Title.

FC3694.25.F47A3 2008   c818'.5409   c2007-906074-9

Editor for the Board: Anne Nothof
Cover and interior design: Natalie Olsen
Cover image: Jessie Ferguson
Author photo: arf

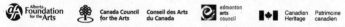

NeWest Press acknowledges the support of the Canada Council for the Arts,
the Alberta Foundation for the Arts, and the Edmonton Arts Council for
our publishing program. We also acknowledge the financial support of the
Government of Canada through the Book Publishing Industry Development
Program (BPIDP).

NeWest Press
201.8540.109 Street
Edmonton, Alberta T6G 1E6
780.432.9427
newestpress.com

No bison were harmed in the making of this book.
We are committed to protecting the environment and to the responsible
use of natural resources. This book is printed on 100% recycled, ancient
forest-friendly paper.

1 2 3 4 5 11 10 09 08   printed and bound in Canada

I was running away.

I had become a person I didn't want to be and, undoing the knot, I quit my job, put a couple of trunks in a storage locker and left the West Coast in a rented car.

Now I was eight hundred miles from Vancouver, driving across northern Alberta on a clear summer morning. My wife and eight-year-old son were beside me. I was taking them to a remote piece of uninhabited bushland we bought by mail, sight unseen. I knew I ought to be worried, but I wasn't. I had a little money in the bank, and when that shallow well dried up, I figured there must be a way I could earn a living—working part-time, maybe, in the nearest town.

Travelling on a gravel road, passing rising crops and grazing cattle, I came to the place I thought might be my financial safety net. Although you can't assess prosperity by looking at a name on a map, I didn't expect Sunnyside to be a gloomy, pot-holed village with three frail businesses lingering in a graveyard of boarded-up stores and offices. If I ever worked there, I would be filling gas tanks, washing beer parlour glasses, or selling bread and milk at Ubanski's General Store.

"Where's the school?" my son, Alex, asked.

"I don't know," my wife, Jessie, answered. "Here somewhere."

I turned off the main drag. Frame bungalows and stucco duplexes collected on quiet side streets. None of them was boarded-up — the shopping mall in the area's biggest town had drained the lifeblood out of Sunnyside's commercial section, but cheap housing prices made the residential district appealing, mostly to retired farmers. At the end of a street, close to an old highway, I drove past a low, brick building that could have fit cozily into an urban industrial park. Sunnyside Elementary.

"You think they'll teach me about dinosaurs?" Alex asked.

P

back
roads
Ted
Ferguson

"Sure. Why not?" I said. "They found a lot of skeletons in this province."

"I know where the dinosaurs disappeared to," he said. "They went to the moon on spaceships."

"Who told you that?"

"Nobody. I thought it up myself."

"If your teachers agree with you," Jessie smiled, "tell me and I'll have you transferred to another school."

Before driving onto the old highway, I re-read the letter that gave directions to our land. Twenty-five miles east of Sunnyside I was to go north on the first road beyond a pink bungalow. The road would end at a swampy ravine; our 160 acres was the last parcel on the left. "Your fence is down, but at least it's there," Susan's letter said. "People tend to swipe barbed wire when land isn't used for a long time. Barbed wire's expensive, and nothing expensive goes to waste in the Alberta outback!"

The highway wasn't used very much. I passed only two cars — black rattletraps travelling miles apart like a divorced couple who couldn't stand looking at each other. The prairie rambled flat and green and practically treeless, and then, a freakish surprise, the pattern was disrupted by a steep hill leading to a thickly wooded plateau known locally as the Dunes. All but a few farmers shunned the region. Compared to the marvellous black earth on the plains, the soil was too poor for growing strong crops. In some spots there were mounds of white sand and short-barrelled Jack pines, but most of the landscape was covered by lakes, bogs, poplars, spruce, and fir. We had been assured there weren't any dunes on our quarter section. We could level the entire property, if we wished, and raise halfway decent crops of oats.

Levelling the land was out of the question. We were going to homestead it. Find an abandoned log cabin and move it onto the site. No electricity, no tap water, a wood-burning stove, and a root cellar. Simplicity and the quintessential Canadian experience: embracing nature. Neither Jessie nor I had lived in the bush, except for holiday visits to her father's Rocky Mountain cabin.

She was a homemaker; I was a journalist. She intended to plant a huge garden and feed whatever livestock we acquired; I intended to cut firewood and dig a well. I counted upon discipline and desire to compensate for the fact that up until that point physical labour for me was helping a mother lift a stroller onto a city bus. Naively or not, I reasoned that the shining joy of living by our own rules on our own land would make any hard work, any bruising obstacle, almost a privilege.

The pink house loomed. Whitewashed tires, separated by stone elves and miniature windmills, rimmed the gravel driveway. The doghouse was plywood; the storage shed was corrugated tin. A weathered flagpole held a "Trespassers Will Be Prosecuted" sign. Issuing a second warning, a hand-printed "Beware of Owner" message was attached to the front door. Whoever occupied the pink house, they had a bog for a backyard.

"Pink is a pacifying colour," Jessie commented. "If it doesn't work on mosquitoes, that house must be swarming with them."

I swung the car onto a dirt road. There were no buildings anywhere, just trees and underbrush and the occasional clearing. Several miles up from the old highway, the road swerved and vanished down a hill. As instructed, I continued going north. I slowed on the bumpy route, which was more of a broad trail than a road. When I reached our property line, I stopped the car and the three of us got out.

It wasn't an inspiring sight. Nothing but poplars half a mile across and, presumably, half a mile deep. I had been hoping for a creek flowing through our yard, or on mild summer nights, a pine grove sending a lovely scent into our home. By the looks of it, I would have to settle for cutting a space in the trees and sticking the cabin in the centre of it.

"Susan said we had a field," Jessie said. "I wonder where it is?"

"I don't know. If it's near the road, we can put the cabin on it."

"She said it wasn't very big."

"Susan's a farmer's daughter, and farmers think 160 acres isn't very big, so anything less than that is minuscule to them."

Leaving Jessie and Alex at the car, I went off to find the field. I followed the collapsed fence that headed down one side of our quarter section. The fenceline divided our land from an identical mass of slender, leafy poplars on the other side. Some of the underbrush came up to my shoulder, but there weren't many trees directly in my path — a rough road, wide enough for a tractor, had once existed there. In the heat and silence, struggling through the bush, I thought of Sunnyside and the "Beware of Owner" sign.

The north country of my imagination — endearing, white-picket communities and welcoming farm families ("Drop in anytime. Coffee's always on the stove.") — was probably an illusion, but I wasn't concerned. I had journeyed here on a kind of spiritual renovation project: to trim away the parts of myself that I didn't like and construct a happier person on the parts that I did. Once we were settled on the homestead it wouldn't matter to us whether dust and cobwebs smothered Sunnyside's main street or if the people in the pink house, unpacified, bit strangers knocking on their door. We planned to be largely self-reliant, taking as little as possible from sources beyond our gate.

The underbrush thinned and, moving more easily, I reached the top of a gradually declining hill. Through the poplars, I could see a portion of a field and, past that, a strip of bluish water. I descended the slope and emerged on a ridge overlooking a long, weedy field that lay parallel to a small lake.

I felt exhilarated, as though I had come upon something rare and precious. A narrow valley rested under the warm sun. It was a place of rolling, wooded hills and grassy clearings. Incredibly, there wasn't a single person, a solitary house, in my line of vision. It was by no means a spectacle as overpowering as the Rockies' stony glory, but it was, in its own gentle manner, a wondrous view. Standing on the ridge, watching ducks rise off the lake, I knew that this was the spot where our cabin was meant to be.

The room I woke up in was dark, stuffy, and cool. I was on the floor, swathed in a sleeping bag, in the windowless bedroom of a turn-of-the-century house that had been lying unoccupied for eight years. One winter evening, the last tenant, a depressive bachelor, made himself a delicious meal of roast beef and Yorkshire pudding and — the finishing touch in its truest form — a cup of Constant Comfort blended with battery acid. The atmosphere must have been a contributing factor to, if not the principal cause of, his decision not to spend another minute on the premises. The scrap lumber walls (mud and straw plugged the gaps), the slivery, two-by-four flooring, and the permanent shadows (the only window in the house was a rectangular opening above the kitchen table) convinced me that the Scottish immigrant who built the house had the aesthetic eye of a ground-burrowing gopher.

"Scary," I heard Alex say in the next room. "Noises all night. Like ghosts."

"It's just the floors whining and groaning because they feel old and tired," Jessie said. "We won't be here forever."

"When will we go?"

"I don't know, sweetheart. When we find our own home."

I crawled out of the sleeping bag, pulled on jeans and a T-shirt, and went into the adjoining kitchen. My wife and son were eating cereal at the card table Susan lent us. I poured myself a coffee and peered outside. The barley looked healthy. It was dense and straight, spreading a great distance. The woman who owned the property, Susan's mother-in-law, Judith Tyson, rented the land to a neighbouring farmer. Arriving at the vacant house at dusk, I hadn't really noticed the crop, or the boulders that generations of sore-back farmers ripped from the earth and heaped along the edge of the field. Judith was a retired high school teacher. She had never planted a crop anywhere, and she never wanted to. Believing the more acreage you possessed the prouder you

1

back
roads
*Ted
Ferguson*

were entitled to be, she bought farmland all over the municipal district, regardless of whether the soil was graded A or D. Once or twice a month, her husband donned a grey polyester suit and chauffeured her to one of the properties, where she walked about, unhurried, indulging her pride.

Jessie and I had met Susan and her husband, Greg, in Mexico years earlier. After they returned to Alberta, we exchanged sporadic letters. When I was on the coast, anguishing over what direction to point my life in, Susan sent a note advising us the municipality was selling a quarter section to cover an unpaid tax bill. Greg's mother wasn't interested, and we could have the land for $2,500. I mailed the money the same week.

While I was gazing at the barley field, Jessie turned from the propane stove and said, "Susan says there's a farmer near Preston with a bulldozer."

"A bulldozer? Why's he got that?"

"Somebody died. An uncle in construction. He left it to him."

"I hereby bequeath my bulldozer to my favourite nephew, my cement mixer to my wife, and a hammer and a keg of nails to my mistress."

"The thing is, he'll clear the road on our land. Susan says he'll do it in a day."

"I've seen the mess bulldozers leave behind. I'd rather do it myself. Carve it out of the woods, like a piece of sculpture. Nothing uprooted. No piles of tangled trees and dirt."

"Okay, I'm willing to try. But if it's too tough a job, we have an alternative."

After breakfast, we drove to the Dunes.

I retrieved a machete and an axe from the car trunk and, stepping to the fenceline, estimated it shouldn't take more than a week to hack a twelve-foot-wide route between the trail-like municipal artery and the ridge where the cabin was going to nestle. Once I had found the cabin, the idea was to number the logs, dismantle the building, haul it down our road and fit it all together again on the site. Other people did it — people with less strength than me — using winches and chains and tripods. My father-in-law was a hunting guide in the Flathead. He was the only person living in the wilds on the Canadian side of the British Columbia–Montana border. On the American side, ultra-conservative ranchers, affluent retirees, potheads, and various social screw-ups dwelt in log homes, grand and modest, scattered about the mountain valley. Joe introduced me to a Vietnam burn-out who dismantled his cabin twice and trucked it elsewhere following disputes with his neighbours. I received the impression that the whole procedure was less trouble than assembling an IKEA bookcase.

Swinging the axe and the machete, I rapidly dispensed with trees and underbrush. After the poplars fell, I chopped them into shorter pieces for Jessie and Alex to lug into the bush. My enthusiasm blazed but my energy dimmed. Within an hour, panting and sweating, I came to realize that I lacked the stamina for a full-throttle rush to the ridge. By the time we quit for the day, around noon, I told myself that even if the road clearing took a month, or longer, I would still do it. I was irrevocably cast in an idealistic role: protector of the woodlands, enemy of the evil bulldozer.

We returned to the shadowy farmhouse for lunch; then we went house hunting. Greg's father, whom we had yet to meet, had written three pages of detailed directions describing the route from Sunnyside to a pair of derelict cabins he spotted between Sunnyside and the shopping mall town, Preston. Without street signs, the backcountry was a puzzling web of criss-crossing roads. I had no problem with directions apprising me to "go east on the second gravel road past the silo with the Maple Leaf painted on it" and "if you're at a bridge, you've missed the turn." However, forgetting he was addressing a stranger to the region, he scribbled a line that was only suitable for long-time local resident: "Head west on the other side of the pasture where John Drysdale grazed his buffalo." Completely stumped, I wheeled into a couple of farmyards before finding somebody who, in explaining exactly where the pasture was, added, "John Drysdale ain't had buffalo for twenty years."

When the first cabin appeared, it looked like something that, losing its value, had been flung aside and shunned. It sat at the far end of a rocky field, so obscured by surrounding willows and brush I wondered how Greg's father determined the building was made of logs. Walking in from the road, our hopes shrank the closer we came. Some of dark brown logs were rotting, and part of the roof had buckled in, likely under the weight of unshovelled snow. Holding willow branches away from my body, I moved to the open doorway and stepped inside. I saw ants and spiders and a dead mouse. The air smelled of mildew. I glanced at the walls. Like a fussy eater, decay had chewed chunks out of several logs.

"Why did Greg's father think we'd be interested in this place?" Jessie asked.

"I don't know," I shrugged. "For firewood?"

From the road, the second cabin Frank directed us to was cloaked in promise. The logs were the silvery-grey colour of aging pine. The roof was even and whole. The building stood in a field adjoining a huge, strictly maintained Victorian house and a recently painted barn. The tractor and the combine resting in the yard were fairly new, contributing to an ambiance of peaceful prosperity. The sign on the fence — "Eggs For Sale"— indicated that the prosperous feeling was not to be trusted. Their spirits bending under the weight of hefty bank loans, many farmers welcomed whatever hard cash they could scrape up, whether it was from selling eggs and rabbits or baby cribs and bicycles.

An ancient, arthritic dog limped to the car when I drove up to the house. It emitted a series of strained barks and yelps, trying to assure us it was still able to mount an effective defense. Alex jumped out and patted its head; the dog silenced itself and flopped to the ground. A plump, middle-aged woman emerged from the house. "Hello there," she said warily.

"Good afternoon," I smiled. "I trust we haven't come at a bad time. We're interested in your cabin."

"What for?"

"To buy it." That was Greg's suggestion: be polite, mention money. Abandoned houses were not uncommon on the Prairies. Especially woodframes. They sat neglected in fields and yards after farmers erected bigger, up-to-date residences. So be polite, mention money, and, nine times out of ten, regarding the empty buildings to be useless, if not embarrassing reminders of humbler days, they'll give them to you free of charge. According to Greg, those odds diminished if you didn't seem like a nice guy and a devoted family man. "The locals may be hurting for dough, but they've got this we're all-in-the-same-boat attitude. A house burns to the ground, they donate food and clothing and toss in a few bucks. Somebody's sick and can't cut a crop, they cut it for him. A guy with a wife and kid asks for an old house — and they like him — they say it's worth sweet bugger-all so that's what he should pay them, sweet bugger-all. Sometimes you meet a farmer who'll feel cheated unless he gets a token: fifty, a hundred bucks. I've heard of a guy swapping a farmhouse for a case of 10W30."

The woman frowned. "It's not for me to say. Talk to my husband."

"Okay. Is he in?"

"He's on his way from town."

Oozing family-man niceness, I asked, "Is it all right if we look at the cabin?"

"Sure, go ahead."

She headed back into the house. The dog drew itself up and limped after her. We walked over to the cabin. Lodgepole pine formed the walls. A sheet of plywood was nailed across the doorway, so we peered through filthy windows. Two rooms, both barren. None of the logs appeared to be decayed.

"This is great," Jessie said.

"Yes. It's perfect."

"Where will I sleep?" Alex asked.

"We'll hire a carpenter to build a room for you," Jessie said. "Anyway, there's no point in planning a renovation until we find out if it's ours."

back
roads
*Ted
Ferguson*

We returned to the car and waited for the owner to show up. Gazing at the cabin, I thought of how beautifully it suited our ridge. I pictured myself standing at the front window, warm and satisfied, watching a blizzard whiten the field. How much should I offer for the cabin? It was a well-crafted gem, and, despite what Greg said, I simply couldn't conceive of the owner signing the building over to us without wanting something worthwhile in return. I was sure he would fall over laughing if I said I'd swap twelve cans of motor oil for it. So what would persuade him? A thousand dollars? Fifteen hundred? I could afford more than that, but the attack on my savings would send me searching for a job by the end of summer.

The cabin owner was short and puffy-faced. He climbed out of a dusty Jimmy holding a bag of groceries.

"Hi there. How's the weather over your way?" he asked.

"Over my way? Good."

"You never can tell. Sunny here and raining someplace else. I'm praying for a bit of rain. No raging storm, mind you. I don't take kindly to flooded fields."

I didn't realize it then, but I was having my initial encounter with a regional custom. Although he must be curious about why three strangers were in his yard, he felt it was impolite to inquire straight off the bat. When someone drove onto your property, they dove into light conversation — the weather, the crops, current affairs — before disclosing the purpose of their visit. Invite them in for coffee and the cups would be drained and you'd be walking to their vehicle when they'd finally say, "The reason I'm here is …" Unaware of the practice, I aborted the weather chatter and announced we'd like to purchase the cabin.

"Can't say I blame you," he said without pausing to consider what I had said. "Lodgepole pine. From the Foothills."

"It's in excellent shape," Jessie said. "When was it built?"

"Thirty-one, thirty-two. 'Round about then. My dad cut the logs. Him and mom put the cabin up, over by Preston. The wife and me hauled it here."

"I have no idea how much to offer you," I said.

"Don't offer me anything."

"No, no, I prefer to pay."

"The cabin isn't for sale."

"But it's deserted. You aren't using it."

"I was born in that cabin."

"How about a thousand dollars? Cash."

"Like I say, I was born in that cabin. I won't sell it, not for a million. There are things close to a man's heart that are more important than money. When there's nothing close to his heart he won't surrender for money, he's a sorry sight for the Lord to lay eyes upon."

I left the yard terribly disappointed. I understood how the owner felt. I was sentimentally attached to objects I'd acquired in my youth: the first classical record I laid hands on (*The Emperor Concerto*) and the first novel that knocked me for a loop (*Native Son*) were in the Vancouver storage locker. Nevertheless, I grumbled, it simply didn't seem right to anchor a log house on a treeless farm dominated by a scene-stealing Victorian and a yardful of modern machinery. It deserved a more natural setting, like a thickly wooded ridge overlooking a lake and a peaceful field. Where it would be inhabited and vibrant; where it wouldn't be a hollow, lifeless relic.

"Stop bitching," Jessie said. "You're a sorry sound for the Lord to lay ears upon. There'll be other cabins. Greg said there were plenty. We have to keep looking."

"Yeah, I guess so. The next one could be nicer. An upper floor, a porch, a fireplace, who knows what."

Greg and Susan's house was in the Dunes, not far from our land. Greg's mother was allowing them to stay in it rent-free — a situation they truly appreciated because neither Greg nor Susan had jobs or intended to get any. They were an engaging couple, intelligent and funny. That didn't mean they were perfect. Greg was unabashedly self-absorbed, and Susan was afflicted with a regrettable propensity to sound like a glued-to-the-Sixties flower child.

"Groovy," she'd say. Or, "Cool it, man." Or, "I can dig it." Laughing at a bizarre story, she'd exclaim, "Outta sight!" She always greeted us with hugs and happy words, and every time we parted she said, "We love you," as if she was giving us candies for being good. I hoarded my candies: one for my wife, one for my son, and none for the couple I barely knew.

Knowing so little about them, we stumbled into the dark areas that hid their demons. Susan's eyes chilled when my wife said Greg's car, a customized Mustang, must have cost him a bundle. On another occasion, Greg referred to a stressful past, hinting he once worked in the medical profession. When I questioned him, he stiffened and then joked his way out of providing a genuine answer. "Was I a doctor? How badly do you want to find out? Get a knife from the kitchen. I'll take out your appendix. I do it correctly, I was a doctor. I take out your liver by mistake, I wasn't."

After the cabin disappointment, dinner at Greg and Susan's was a regenerating event: candles on the table, *Nashville Skyline* on the turntable, wine and lasagna, smiles and laughter.

"We'll look at some more cabins tomorrow," I said, slicing a piece of lasagna. "Where should we go?"

"I'll ask my father," Greg said.

"You haven't spotted any yourself?"

"Greg doesn't leave the Dunes," Susan answered for him. "There are no log houses around here."

"You don't leave the Dunes?" I said to Greg, somewhat surprised.

"Susan does the shopping. I haven't been to town since last year — my mother's birthday."

"That's the only time he goes," Susan said. "On her birthday."

"Why's that?" Jessie asked.

Greg shrugged his shoulders and Susan replied, "No special reason. He doesn't like Preston." "How big's the mall?" Alex broke in. "You think they've got Marvel comics?"

"Maybe," Susan said. "The supermarket has magazines. I haven't noticed comic books."

Minutes later, the record player having fallen silent, we heard a beeping horn. Greg jumped up and crossed to a window.

"My father," he said disagreeably. "He's got somebody's truck."

"Whose?" Susan asked.

"Never saw it before."

Greg plunked onto his chair and resumed eating. A man wearing a flannel shirt and Cougar boots ambled through the front door. They didn't look like father and son. Greg was lean, long-legged, and fine-featured, while Frank Tyson was a deep-chested individual with broad cheekbones and large, powerful-looking hands.

"Am I interrupting?"

"Sorry but you can't join us," Susan said. "I didn't make enough."

Frank nodded towards Jessie and me. "You must be the Fergusons. Glad to meet you. I'm Greg's dad. Don't go calling me Mr. Tyson. Frank's the name. How are you folks doing?"

"Fine," Jessie retorted.

"They say Vancouver's awfully polluted."

"They're right," I said.

"With sea breezes, you'd figure the smog wouldn't settle."

"It's the mountains and the rain clouds," Jessie said. "The smog's trapped."

"That so? We don't get pollution in these parts. The air's as pure as a baby's beating heart."

He was standing behind Susan, watching us eat. Evidently that was bothering her. She swung her head and said, "Why don't you sit down? There's some *Geographics* on the couch."

Frank went to the couch. A bulky eyesore, it was a parting gift from the man who sold Judith the property. A bottle depot manager, he built the house himself using how-to books and the services of a glass-eyed, partially deaf friend. The final product was a small, bland, irritatingly flawed house. Doors wouldn't shut and windows wouldn't open. Closet shelves collapsed and the roof leaked. The bathroom sink and the upstairs ceiling were absurdly low. Frank did minor repairs and removed the wall between the

back roads
Ted Ferguson

kitchen and the parlour to make the ground floor area feel roomier. He taped the light switch wiring to an adjacent wall, hoping to meet an electrician who'd tell him what to do with it. Greg preferred having the couch face the kitchen. He was an amateur woodcarver — his foot-high, figurative pieces decorated the house — and he could sit bent over the coffee table, chiselling and sanding and speaking to his wife while she cooked. Now, with his father talking and ignoring the *Geographics*, Greg looked as though he was about to leap up and start rebuilding the wall.

Frank spoke slowly, not because he was assessing his sentences, fearful of saying the wrong thing, but, it occurred to me weeks later, because he was never in a hurry to go anywhere or do anything. He tended to his wife's properties, fixing fences and killing gophers. He had no close friends and he was obligated to be by himself most of the day, but he was a born talker who let his tongue out of the cage, running and jumping, whenever possible. As we proceeded from the main course to dessert, Frank rendered his opinion on hockey ("It's like ballet, except the ballet dancers don't get artistic temperament and pound each other."), federal politics ("That damn Trudeau acted like he was a king. He oughta worn a crown and gone around knighting people."), and bears ("The sure way of knowing a grizzly from a black bear is if it's tearing your head off it's a grizzly."). He was starting in on Hutterites as we finished the meal.

"Everybody says they don't fit in. If they'd put their kids in the Little Cowhands Rodeo or signed up for tire-rolling at Frontier Daze, they'd be accepted. You don't support community events, folks in Preston are apt to pull in their welcome mats."

"Unfortunately, that's a universal condition," I said.

"I imagine it is. You want to come outside for a minute? While Susan's brewing coffee, I'll show you the truck I brought."

"He isn't interested in a bloody truck," Greg snapped.

"I recall you saying he's eager to buy a vehicle so he can unload the rental car."

"Oh. I forgot."

"The situation hasn't changed has it?"

"No."

"Then I'll show him the truck."

"Whose truck is it?"

"Mine."

Frank led me into the yard. A black Chevy pickup was parked in front of the barn. It wasn't a matter of love at first sight. The windshield was splintered, the hood scratched, and the passenger door bashed. An abused product that, I gathered, rolled off a Michigan assembly line in the 1960s. Yet I realized almost immediately that the Chevy, though it would never be loved, suited my image of the sort of vehicle a contemporary homesteader should drive: a body-scarred plain Jane challenging the urban concept that motor vehicles ought to be gleaming show wagons.

"I did the rings and brakes on a junkyard Ford," Frank said. "Instead of money, I took the Chevy. All it needed was grease and a radiator hose."

"Can I drive it?"

"Sure. I'll go with you. We have to stay clear of the highway — no plates, no insurance."

The truck rode smoothly. Frank pledged that if I ever had any problems with it he would rectify them without charge. He had been a service station mechanic, but he said he quit to "take care" of his wife, making it sound as though she was an invalid.

"How much are you selling the truck for?" I asked.

"Two hundred."

"Terrific."

Wheeling the Chevy into the yard, I told him the cabins he directed me to hadn't worked out.

"Is that a fact?" he said. "Well, I can't recall seeing others. Your best bet's to drive up and down back roads. They couldn't have hauled them all off to heritage museums."

back
roads
Ted
Ferguson

2

There had to be a town somewhere in Canada that rejected the seductive call of strident commercialism. A town where the rulers chose hushed beauty over loud and trite when deciding the fate of the highway strip leading into their community. A town with trees and gardens flourishing along the entry route among waterfalls and walkways, fountains and ponds. Where peacocks wandered and swans floated and strolling citizens paused for reflective moments in handsome gazebos. If such a place existed, it wasn't Preston. The highway conveying us into the town was edged by a clotted mess of sales-pitch signs and box-inspired architecture. Mister Doughnut stared across the asphalt lanes at a Go-Kart track. A purple-striped hamburger outlet faced a used car lot permanently festooned with blinking Christmas lights.

Once we passed through the strip and reached the downtown area, Preston was a fairly pleasant place. Not exceptionally pretty — not like communities of a similar size in Nova Scotia and Vermont — but the main street, Palliser, did accommodate a number of leafy maples, daffodil-laden planters, and attractive brick buildings constructed early in the twentieth century. We rode by a public library, a movie theatre, a municipal swimming pool, and a second-hand book store. The mall had clamped a near-fatal stranglehold on Sunnyside and other outlying centres, but rather than harming Preston, the out-of-towners' spillover business permitted Palliser Street to breathe easy.

We were running errands: acquiring plates and insurance for the truck, renting a post office box, grocery shopping, doing laundry, and, an absolute necessity for me, visiting McDonald's Pharmacy to pick up Aspirin and Absorbine Jr. I had enjoyed the first day of road building, feeling as though I were beginning a new phase of masculine development, entering the Brotherhood of Manly Men. Before we drove to Preston, I woke up in the morning forced to pay the initiation fee: I wandered the farm-house with slow, unwillingly motions — head throbbing, muscles and bones playing a fugue of pain and misery.

Begging relief, I opened the Aspirin bottle on the sidewalk outside the drugstore and swallowed pills without a liquid chaser. We got the plates and insurance and the post box, and then we motored to the mall. It was spacious and square and, like the highway strip, strikingly charmless. While Jessie and Alex bought groceries and comic books, I went to the laundromat.

I tacked a slip of paper to the notice board: "Log cabin wanted. Must be in livable condition. Will move to different location. Please reply to box 1208, Preston."

A forty-something blonde with curlers in her hair witnessed the posting. She inserted a coin in a dryer, raised a crimson-nailed hand to chain-light a cigarette, and, reaffirming my sup-position that anything new appearing in a rural community was a beguiling object, she walked to the board.

"You'll be lucky," she scoffed.

"I'm counting on it."

"They weren't keen on log houses around here. Trees were rare as hen's teeth. Some people did build them, though."

"Have you seen any?"

"The Hewisons. The Poison Creek Hewisons — no relation to the gang over by Sunnyside — they've one, but it's rotted to ruin. You know what's best? Have a company in Edmonton ship you a prefab. Real Simple Simon. You snuggle the logs together."

"No, that isn't for me."

"Please yourself," she said, returning to her wash.

I had already considered and dismissed prefabricated log houses. Extremely expensive, and they didn't quite look right to me — all that fresh, neatly rounded timber was the wilderness version of identical subdivision homes. I had sent for a prefab cat-alogue after scrapping my original scheme to build my own cabin. Upon learning that our quarter section was mostly covered by trees, I had borrowed a library book written in the 1960s when

back roads
Ted Ferguson

[25]

the back-to-the-land movement blew across the North American landscape like a cleansing wind. The author and her boyfriend fled Los Angeles to build a house in northern BC. It took them two summers to drag appropriately straight logs to the site and construct the house. Somewhere in the text the writer expressed her gratitude for the monthly inheritance cheques supplying food and gas and other staples. I wouldn't have two summers to build a house or legacy cheques brightening my mail box. I embraced the idea of dismantling and raising a cabin when the Vietnam vet asserted that even a greenhorn like me could accomplish the job in four to six weeks.

The laundromat notice failed to yield a single letter. Neither did an advertisement in the *Preston Gazette*, nor the item on "Shamrock Plumbing's Community Corral," which the regional station had been broadcasting five times a week at 11:05 AM for "thirty-three good-neighbour years."

A routine settled upon us: mornings we cleared the road, afternoons we scoured the countryside. Alex became bored with the ritual and issued a statement that astounded us; he wished it was September so he could go to school. Criss-crossing the farmlands, we saw intriguing houses: a masterly example of nineteenth-century frilliness (cupola, gingerbread, and turrets), a converted barn with stained glass windows, and, considerably less humble than either of those, a flat-roofed abode combining beer bottles, mud, and straw. We also saw derelict houses, but none of them was made of logs.

My confidence was cracking. I continued to claim aloud that we'd eventually discover a great cabin if we stubbornly stuck to the hunt, even though we might have to travel twenty or thirty miles in every direction. Secretly, as the weeks slipped by, I was disturbed by sudden surges of doubt and guilt. I had uprooted my wife and child in pursuit of a personal vision that I was starting to suspect was naive and possibly slightly crazy. How much longer could I go on like this? Building a road to a weedy field, staying in a grim farmhouse, sleeping on hard floors knowing that if we were still there next winter we would be dependent on space heaters and a truckload of heavy clothing to spare us a frozen death. And if I ran away from the problem, where would I run to? Four hours after I resigned from the Vancouver newspaper, the managing editor, who said I was a uniquely talented columnist he'd have difficulty replacing, appointed a replacement. Leaving northern Alberta and taking a journalism job in Edmonton or another city meant opening a colourfully wrapped package and learning the same undesirable product was stuffed inside.

One stiflingly hot day, the road more than half finished, I left Jessie and Alex eating luncheon sandwiches and walked to the back of our property. There was a large boulder at the top of the field, near the spot where I wanted the cabin to nestle. I sat on the rock and surveyed the valley. The lake glittered fetchingly and the hills dipped and rose with easy grace, but it was the field on my property that appealed to me the most. Facing west, it slanted gently down to confront the bulrushes and marshy shoreline that made the lake inaccessible. Turning my head, I gazed north to appreciate the way the field gradually tilted upwards, starting roughly around the middle and stopping at a barrier of poplars standing on the Crown land next to mine. I delighted in its shape and texture, the verdant greenness and the thin row of willow and chokecherry trees clustered along the fenceline between it and the lake. To view the landscape from an altered perspective I descended the slope. At the bottom, I spied something I was previously unaware of. A slender band of grassland on the Crown quarter section to the south reached from my busted and bruised barbed wire fence to the edge of an enclosed field that, defying the Dunes' mediocre-crop reputation, was dense with barley.

I looked up the slope.

Once again, I envisaged a cabin lodged twenty yards back from the field, a bank of trees defending it against drifting snow. It didn't seem like a wild-minded dream; it seemed a certainty, a rendering of benevolent fate. On the West Coast I felt like an actor playing a role I couldn't relate to. My daily behaviour was — as

Shakespeare might have put it if he was writing today — kicking the crap out of my inner peace. I suffered from insomnia, dizziness, skin rashes, and a suddenly acquired fear of heights. I still had difficulty getting to sleep, but the other symptoms disappeared. I had to continue the transformation; I had to go on searching for a home and ignore the doubt and guilt.

The routine continued: chopping, slashing, cabin-hunting.

As the summer advanced, the heat intensified. There were two schools of opinion concerning whether or not this was a fine thing. The husband and wife proprietors of Ubanski's General Store in Sunnyside and the townsfolk I encountered in Preston shops raved about the weather. Farmers fretted over the lack of rain, and the fact that when it did come it quickly ceased. At the mall a farmer shook his head and lamented, "It's like snatching a glass of water from a fella in a desert after he's drunk a mouthful."

The hot days persuaded us to add a third element to our ritual: a late-afternoon visit to the Dunes' swimming hole. Mirror Lake drew people from Preston and surrounding flatlands before the municipal pool opened. Concrete, chlorine, and crowding were evidently more alluring than Jack pines, lily pads, and cool, fresh water. We always had Mirror Lake to ourselves, except for the times Susan and Greg showed up.

One afternoon, the four of us were lazing on the bushy shoreline. *Blue Bayou* was in the air. The Chevy had an eight-track player beneath the dashboard, and in a cardboard box at the Sally Ann, Susan had discovered a batch of cassettes. The truck was parked behind us and Alex, temporarily enthralled, was popping the cassettes in and out of the machine, spurning Willie Nelson, hugging Linda Ronstadt.

"Greg doesn't like Willie Nelson either," Susan said. "And he used to be a cowboy."

"I wasn't a real cowboy," Greg said. "I was wrangling for a Rocky Mountain outfit. You know, trail-riding tourists."

"The wages were shitty," Susan said. "Minimum wage. But the fringe benefits were groovy—he slept with a hundred girls."

"Thirty-eight," Greg said matter-of-factly. "I planned on wrangling till I hit one hundred, but the outfit went belly up."

"City girls are crazy for wranglers," Susan said. "They have this idea they're romantic figures. Strong, quiet."

"They're definitely quiet," Greg said. "They're stupid, and by the time they form a sentence in their head, you've left for the day."

"You had plenty to say when you were doing it."

"Yeah, and most of it was lies. I'd tell women they rode magnificently, like equestrian champions, even if they were flopping all over the horse. I'd say their horse really adored them, that a unique communication was taking place. Sometimes phony flattery, or saying a bloody word, wasn't necessary. I was cleaning a stall at the lodge and this chick from New York I didn't talk to on the trail waltzes in. She says her boyfriend's in the pub and then she throws herself at me. I guess she thought that was romantic, humping in horseshit."

"I was so lucky to marry Greg," Susan said, rising to go for a swim. "Everybody wanted him."

Susan's declaration didn't sit well with me. Not what she said—although I did feel most females might consider a score-keeping womanizer a rotten catch—but her worshipful tone. As if Greg, an ordinary specimen to me (and Jessie), walked on water while the rest of us males needed lifeguards. Low self-esteem, I concluded, grasping the instant diagnosis popularized by talk show psychologists. Susan had an affection-famished childhood on an over-populated farm (five brothers, four sisters) and she was by no means happy with the BA she earned at the University of Alberta. It was an achievement that allowed her to follow the career path lit by innumerable BA-holders: waitressing in a hotel bar. She wasn't pretty, but her Slavic face—the huge, brown eyes and the full, expressive mouth—were more sensual, more compelling, than a runway model's cold perfection. I doubted Susan pictured herself in those terms. Tell a woman who isn't drop-dead gorgeous that she's wonderful to look at and she'll distrust everything you say about her from that moment on.

Susan did, however, think highly of her breasts: the silent seducers she carried into the world under deep-swooping blouses and tight tank tops. "What's your favourite part of your body?" she asked my wife during a town trip. "I don't have a favourite part," Jessie retorted. "It's all the same to me." "Mine's my boobs. Women envy them and men go nuts trying to please me. I've gotten discounts in stores, and guys bring me stuff from home they don't use anymore. Like our dishes and lawn chairs." Observing her wading into the lake, I ruminated that despite the ebullient assurance she constantly projected, Susan perceived in her heart-of-hearts that her breasts — and living with Greg — were the only things she had going for her.

"You people must be sick of house hunting," Greg said as Linda Ronstadt progressed to "Hurts So Bad."

"Are we ever," Jessie sighed.

"Our fault. Susan was optimistic in my letters. Sorry about that, but we really did think there must be a ton of log cabins available. Anyway, Susan and I were surprised that you actually came here. We thought you bought the land for an investment. We didn't expect you to leave your comfortable life in Vancouver."

"It wasn't that comfortable," I muttered.

"It was my mother's idea to tell you the land was for sale. She was busy landing a condo in the city. She figured on having you buy the quarter and then down the road she'd offer a bit more than you paid."

"Your mother has a condo?" Jessie queried.

"Yeah. She's leasing it to a dentist. My grandfather owned four or five businesses in Preston. He left her his money and she saves like a miser. Practically every penny crossing my mother's palm is funnelled into property. Peanuts in the bank, but on paper she's the richest lady in the municipal district."

Two or three nights later, Greg's father drove into our yard. He [
had been dropping by regularly since we were introduced to him,
usually timing his visits to coincide with Jessie's dinner prepara-
tions. We didn't mind feeding him. He was good-natured and self-
effacing, and besides, a few meals a week were worth exchanging
for the information he supplied, such as enlightening us that the
Hutterite colony sold ten-pound sacks of carrots and potatoes well
below the supermarket price.

"Isn't this swell weather?" Frank said, entering the house. "Sun
in the morning and sun in the afternoon. Cottonballs for clouds.
Big, fat cottonballs."

"Yes, it's swell," Jessie said. "Hot but not sticky. I hate humidity."

"It don't go humid here. The Lord's in our camp. The sticky
city, Toronto, the Lord punishes them for caring for nothing but
sex and shopping. So how's the truck treating you?"

"No problems," I said.

"The Black Bobcat," Alex said. "That's what we call it."

"Why's that?" Frank asked.

"The truck's black and my dad saw a cat he said was a stray.
We wanted a cat for catching mice, so my mom went into the
bushes saying, 'Here, kitty-kitty,' and when she came up to it she
ran out real fast because it was a bobcat."

Frank chuckled and said, "I bet your mom's glad it didn't attack
her. You know something, Alex, the municipality's building you
a road."

"What road?" I asked.

"The law says the school bus has to come within half a mile of
a pupil's home. The municipality reckoned the road to your land
was too narrow and bumpy, so they're building you one. Wide
and graded. With a place near your gate for the bus to turn. I ran
into the surveyors south of here. They said the road will be ready
by September."

"Thank goodness for that," Jessie said. "We were worried about
going up and down that trail in the winter."

We gathered at the dinner table. As usual, Frank discussed a story he heard on the news and then, determining he had waited long enough, he suddenly said, "I've found a house for you."

"A log house?" Jessie asked.

"You strip the siding off, it's logs."

The house was thirty miles from the Dunes. It was selling for six hundred dollars. A three-bedroom structure: one downstairs, two upstairs. No need to dismantle the building; for twelve hundred dollars, a local mover would haul it to our land intact.

"I can't do that," I said. "The road I'm making isn't wide enough."

"Forget your road," Frank said confidently. "You know the barley field on the far side of the Crown quarter? Your ace-in-the-hole. All you have to do is talk the owner into letting you cross it."

The owner lived in the Dunes, ten miles west of us. He gave Jessie and me coffee and cake in his kitchen, and without a moment's hesitation he also gave us permission to transport anything we cared to transport over his land — after the barley was cut and thrashed and heading to the elevator. So we bought the six-hundred-dollar house and waited for summer to unravel. The mover — chunky, personable Will Chumak — expressed concern that the building might prove to be too heavy to winch onto his thirty-year-old Dodge flatbed truck. Jessie calmly adapted to the news, but I went into the chamber and tortured myself. I worried about the winch and about the weather turning unforgivably cruel (an abnormally early winter, snow burying everything) and about the Mounties. Chumak, a farmer who earned extra dollars hauling buildings, hated filling out forms and paying fees; he refused to apply for a municipal moving permit or to contract hydro workers to lift any wires he may have to pass under. What if a patrolling Mountie sighted us halfway to the Dunes and confiscated the building?

The house — a cute, white woodframe in superb condition — had marvellous hardwood floors, knotty-pine cabinets, and an oak staircase off the living room, the centre steps rubbed down by decades of footwear. What it didn't have was furniture. Not a solitary piece. We expected to eventually strip the siding off the house, and, agreeing that antique furnishings would be more compatible with our new lifestyle than modern, we went to farm auctions, some in small communities outside Preston, where they were held weekly, and others on distant farms where, stunned by bankruptcy, morose families clustered in the background to witness the disposal of their possessions. The prices fit our budget: a wood-burning Commodore stove for twenty dollars; a pot-bellied, Winnipeg coal-burner for thirty-five dollars; a French-Canadian pine armoire for sixty dollars; a crank-handle Pathe gramophone

3

back
roads
*Ted
Ferguson*

[33]

for seventeen dollars. When summer fell apart and the barley was gone, it rained. Drizzling, ground-mucking, frustrating rain. Days and days of it. Delayed beyond the date he intended to begin working on our house, Chumak turned to a project that didn't depend on dry weather. When the rain stopped and the earth hardened, I called him from a booth in Preston.

"Can't make her this week," he said. "I'm renovating my father-in-law's kitchen. Relax. Take her easy. We don't do your house before winter, we'll do her first thing next spring."

"Next spring?" I groaned. "Please don't say that."

"Next spring's a breeze," he said, aiming to placate me. "I've had a guy wait three years."

Days later, Judith Tyson sent word through her husband that we could inhabit the farmhouse free of charge until we were settled on the homestead, no matter how many months that took. We appreciated the gesture, but the notion of spending a whole winter marking time in a bleak, frigid dwelling was distressing. If we had to suffer through what the *Preston Gazette* was predicting would be an exceptionally cold season, we wanted to suffer in our own place!

Two weeks passed, and then Chumak came by the farmhouse to announce, "Unless she rains, we'll start moving her Tuesday."

She didn't rain. On a cool September morning, we assembled at the house we bought. The dairy farmer selling it to us had built an aluminum-sided duplex nearby. His sheep dog slept inside the vacant house.

"That old bugger's gonna bite you the day it dawns on him you're evicting him," Chumak said, nodding toward the hairy animal suspiciously observing us.

"I'll bring a bone to give him when he realizes it."

"Don't trouble yourself," Chumak's helper chuckled. "He's already picked out a bone — your leg."

I helped the two men unload shovels, jacks, and wooden blocks from the flatbed. I sliced my finger on a shard of broken glass, a minor cut, and I swore loudly and insisted I didn't need

Polysporin because swearing loudly and insisting you didn't need Polysporin was how working men reacted when they damaged themselves. For six days, the three of us dug under the building, jacked it up, and installed the blocks. On the seventh day, the bottom of the house sitting level with the flatbed, Chumak wrapped chains around it, placed steel rollers between the flatbed and the house, and hooked up a winch.

"This'll be an education," Chumak's helper said.

The motor roared and strained and nothing happened. Chumak tried again. The house shifted — less than an inch, but it shifted.

"Whatever you're cooking for supper," he said to Jessie, "it seems to me you'll be cooking it on your own land."

We followed the house in the Black Bobcat. Jessie was excited; I was tense (the building might snap the chains on an upgrade and slide off the truck), and Alex, happy to be fleeing the spooky, near-windowless farmhouse, was singing and popping cassettes in and out of the eight-track.

Chumak crept along back roads, pausing to check the chains and to raise a hydro wire with a wooden pole. Approaching the Dunes, Chumak edged onto the old highway. A vehicle appeared — a camper, not a police cruiser. The Dodge climbed the hill, passed the pink house, and, taking a seldom used dirt road, crossed the crop-less barley field. When the truck eased onto our property I felt the tension flow out of me. We were safe. We were home.

The next morning I awakened early. The light was a timid yellow, like [a tinted frame in a Hollywood movie. Jessie called me into the living room. A white-tailed deer stood in the clearing in front of the house. It was a lovely sight, a house-warming gift from Mother Nature.

We went into the kitchen. We had collected deadwood the previous night to cook breakfast on the Commodore. Jessie lit the fire and I peered at the stove, wondering how we would endure the looming winter with deadfall and coal, no running water, no electricity, and a frail bank balance.

4

I may have been fooled by Sunnyside's ill-suited name, but New Hamburg was essentially the town the road map implied it was: a hatchery for Germanic sensibilities. There was a German bakery, a German meat market, a German clothing store, and a German auto dealership. The mayor was named Buchhold; the brother and sister trombonists fronting the dance hall band were the Krugers. With such an ethnic overload, I motored through New Hamburg to the Harmony Coal Company prepared to encounter a slew of iron-limbed Aryan men.

There weren't any Aryan men. Only nuns. Driving trucks, climbing ladders, working the chute, fixing a generator, operating strip-mine machinery. The nuns wore black, but they had tinkered with the Vatican dress code. Their habits were shortened into knee-length garments, permitting the wearers freer movement, and an emblem was emblazoned over the breast, a gold arrow piercing a scarlet heart. Some of the women favoured jeans under their habits; others preferred dark-coloured slacks. Sneakers and work boots were the footwear choices. The nuns all appeared to be moving slowly, as though the penalty for haste was stake burning.

"What order do these ladies belong to," Jessie mused, "the Congregation of the Sacred Lump?"

A nun with horsey teeth motioned for me to back the Black Bobcat up to the chute that rose to the summit of a coal heap. Her companion — superb teeth, a horsey nose — loaded the box. The Black Bobcat showed its age. The springs moaned and the tires sank like an obese senior plopping onto a deep-cushioned sofa. I went into the office. More nuns were answering the phone, writing invoices, and licking envelopes. A knobby, grey-haired man, his sawed-off black robe over an open-neck shirt and patched jeans, came to the counter.

"Hello, my friend," he said in a throaty voice transmitting a

French accent. "I'm Brother Henri. It's smart, buying your coal today. Winter's staring us in the face."

"I hope not."

"Flurries in Fort McMurray yesterday. How far do you live from here?"

"Thirty miles, more or less."

Brother Henri grinned, shook his head. "Oh boy, you can't be from New Hamburg. We don't talk miles in this corner of the world. People got confused by the federals ramming kilometres up their snouts. Some still counted by miles; some counted by kilometres. So we all agreed, silently — a psychic connection — to judge distances in minutes. A fellow wrote in the newspaper that road signs should read, 'eighty-six minutes to Preston, six hours and forty-two minutes to Winnipeg.'"

"In that case, I'm forty minutes away. More or less."

"Close. Phone the next time and Brother Henri will deliver. Save the wear and tear on your vehicle."

"I'll do that."

At the pickup, the horsey-toothed nun was leaning in the window, speaking to Jessie. She straightened and turned and said, "I was saying to your wife you'll be clamouring for more coal before winter's done. She said she knows, it goes to twenty below. I told her twenty's a blessing. At fifty below, twenty's a day in Hawaii."

On the way home, driving slower than a coal yard nun, I asked Jessie what else she and the woman had talked about.

"The order's name. It's taken from an obscure fourteenth-century sect: The Servants of the Adored Blood."

"You're kidding. Is that what they call themselves?"

"So she said. They've broken away from the official church because it's too lenient."

"Which policies are too lenient? Abortion or adultery?"

"Most of the nuns are from Quebec. The only male in the order is the character who started it."

"Brother Henri. I met him in the office."

Was that as strange as it seemed, or were there actually other congregations of nuns where the Mother Superior was a man? And what kind of man was he? A brilliant theologian like Martin Luther, whose spark ignited a new global religion, or an angry lunatic bound to do nothing extraordinary beyond recruiting a pack of presumably normal women to his cause? Brother Henri didn't seem crazy but, I conceded, Caligula probably lounged in the emperor's box at the Coliseum, discussing the changing season, travel distances, and the necessity of storing coal in his villa before the cold winds blew.

By late September, under the cover of darkness, frost began paying regular visits to our land, colouring the leaves and establishing a chill that lasted all day. Everyone said we were lucky it hadn't snowed yet, an opinion we gratefully shared, for winter's slow start provided additional preparation time. Outside, we put up the storm windows that came with the house and dragged dead poplars to a firewood pile. Inside, we attached weather stripping around the exterior doors and installed a propane lighting fixture in the kitchen. Until we dug a well in the spring, obtaining water would be a continual nuisance. The green plastic barrel beside the stove had to be filled by hauling five-gallon containers from Susan and Greg's well and the mall laundromat. We obtained a pair of sleds, intending to park the truck near the municipal road during the winter, inside the wide, wooden gate we salvaged from a town dump, and slide the water to our house.

On those crisp fall mornings, shortly after breakfast, Alex and I walked past the truck, stationed behind the house, and went up the hill for the hike to the road the municipality built for him. My road, the one I obstinately carved along the fenceline, was too rough for the school bus to negotiate. Those morning walks were, I thought, a reward for all those decades of riding the urban rollercoaster. Amid the yellows and reds of autumn, tree tops bending to reach over us like paint-smudged fingers, we heard birds singing, we spied a moose — huge, nonchalant, awesomely beautiful —

going through the woods, and more than once, no matter how quietly we approached its nest, we caused a great horned owl to rise off the summit of a tall poplar, fly aggressively in our direction, and then veer into the bush. Late in the afternoon, concerned that a bear or a similarly uncivil animal might regard a skinny child as an easy meal, I met the school bus at the gate for a walk home filled with conversations about "okay" teachers, hard subjects, and "stupid" pupils. "A kid in my class is so stupid," Alex swore, "he failed sandbox and repeated kindergarten."

Sometimes, desiring a break from the essential chores, I climbed the hill in mid-afternoon and entered the woods to look for an object that likely didn't exist. Somebody told Frank that somebody else heard that many years ago a deer hunter had found a natural spring in the middle of our quarter section. I criss-crossed the land, following no particular pattern, and ostensibly looked for a source of pure, constantly flowing water. When you got right down to it, I was really tramping about the woods for the pleasure of being there. I loved the sense of solitude, the sound of a brisk wind shaking the leaves, dislodging the weak and withery. Like all wilderness tracts, mine hid its charms. Glancing at it from the road, the landscape looked empty, dull, just trees and rocks and underbrush. A false face dissuading human intruders; like a sultan and his harem, it was trying to keep its delights to itself. With a form of curiosity that had lain discarded longer than I could recall — a child's feeling of awe — I studied ant hills and spider webs, moss and oddly coloured stones, the way shrinking afternoon light laced a grassy clearing, the puzzling existence of a lone geranium in a stony gully. While I was crouching, picking mushrooms, a coyote, the most elusive of all prairie bush dwellers, passed within several feet of me, cautious eyes fixed on a broad thicket, its generally efficient nose failing to catch my scent.

Left alone in nature, people reflect on their personal lives, their triumphs and shortcomings, their current status. At least that's what they tend to do in novels. Authors install characters in alpine meadows or on lonely, seaside beaches, and an interlude of

back roads
Ted Ferguson

introspective rumination produces a new understanding, perhaps a life-altering decision. Nothing like that happened to me. No revelations, no directional resolutions. I stared into the future, a misty, shifting realm at best, and distinguished the outline of the territory I was attempting to reach, the island where I would be at peace with myself. The past, particularly the recent past, received limited scrutiny. It was discomforting to recall the stress and confusion, the horrible night I dropped to the floor in a posh Vancouver restaurant and, in front of my wife and a couple of friends, sat there until I was pulled up and assisted to the elevator.

] Winter announced its arrival with a whisper, not the shout I had anticipated. Dawn flurries committed the valley to a patchy covering scarcely thicker than the plastic sheeting shielding the coal pile. The lake looked abandoned. The ducks and the geese had sped to the southern border, considering the risk of taking a hunter's bullet a wiser choice than freezing their tailfeathers. The beavers stayed put, hunkering down in sturdy shelters, and unless a bleeding-heart animal-welfare advocate was putting them up in his home for the winter, the muskrats and frogs were also hanging tough.

"The lake's shallow," Jessie said, standing by the kitchen window. "It will freeze to the bottom. We can skate on it."

"That'll be great. We're short on milk and sugar. You want to go to town?"

Jessie collected her jacket. She said nothing, but her expression told me what she was thinking. I had been going to Preston a lot lately. She knew I had submitted story ideas for freelance writing assignments and, anxious to check the mail, I was burning costly gas. By cutting corners, we had stretched our savings beyond the point where I originally figured they would be erased. Now, even if we ate one meal a day and took less fuel-consuming trips to town, I was three weeks away from having to find a job. Sunnyside was off the employment map for me. Unlike many Canadian males, I hated the smell of beer parlours; the service station was a declining, one-man operation; and the husband and wife running Ubanski's General Store apprised me that they didn't make enough profit to hire a helper. The school was advertising for a janitor, but Alex, dreading ridicule, said he'd be mortified if the kids in his class saw me cleaning up the dog shit somebody tracked into the building. Preston's weekly newspaper held the premier position on my job-hunt list. I would urge the editor to employ me to produce stories similar to the sparkler in a recent edition, "Local Senior Makes Handbags."

A letter lying in my post office box eliminated that possibility. A national magazine was accepting two story proposals. With no rent to pay, we could live for a long time on the fees. We celebrated at the finest eatery in town, a drive-in hamburger stand, and then we bought something we had postponed buying until I hooked onto a money source, a high-calibre, battery-powered cassette radio. The spending spree over, we stopped at the Co-op store to pick up a blade for my swede saw — I constantly twisted and snapped the damn things jamming them in trees.

Wally was on duty. Wally Glossop — thin, balding, fiftyish — was the acting assistant manager widely known as Wally Gossip. As numerous writers have pointed out in the past, and as numerous others will reiterate in the future, gossip flows through small-town Canada like a life-sustaining fluid. Wally was a tireless collector and distributor, a master of the under-appreciated craft. He tried to harvest information out of everyone he came across: in the store, on the street, at the bowling alley, wherever potential sources materialized. Faithful friends, and there were many, reportedly dropped by the Co-op solely to contribute items about illicit affairs and sad divorces, car crashes and wicked bush parties: the usual slate of rural tragedy and misconduct. Aware that telling Wally anything meant telling it to half the town, I strictly monitored my end of our conversations and, to amuse Jessie, I occasionally mixed him a cocktail of fact and fiction. Learning he loyally dispatched financial donations to a smarmy television preacher, I said that I was once a television critic and that I had gone to a plush hotel suite to interview the evangelist (fact) and accidentally caught an adolescent blonde in a frilly slip rendering a mouth-to-mouth bubble gum transfer (fiction).

The TV evangelist tale was a rotten idea. Wally, whom I preferred to avoid, enjoyed it so much that, spotting me on the premises, he always came in my direction. One day he was preoccupied with a fussy customer and I made it to the cash register with a case of motor oil, only to have Wally scoot over and insist on pushing the Co-op cart to the truck. In the parking lot, ears starving for a verbal snack, he inquired, "What's brewing out your way?"

So I almost expected it when Jessie and I were scouring the saw blade section and Wally Gossip popped up in the aisle.

"What are you after?"

"A swede saw blade. Eighteen inches."

"Hmmm, none here. I'm sure we've got them." He gestured towards a frumpy clerk in kitchen appliances and called out, "Sonia, will you be a good girl and round up a swede blade in the back. Eighteen inch." Facing us again, he commented, "Sonia's a big asset for the Co-op. She knows the store like the palm of her hand. Didn't marry. Some say she's keen on women, if you catch my drift, but I say that can't be, she wears make-up. What are you using your saw for? Oh, cutting deadwood. Chainsaw's are a darnsight faster. No, no, nothing to be nervous of. A chainsaw can't hurt you unless you're careless. How's everything in the Dunes? No problems? Here comes Sonia." Accompanying us to the cash register, Wally surprised me — cognizant of his data-gathering proficiency, I shouldn't have been surprised — by revealing he knew that Jessie and I had befriended Greg and Susan in Mexico. "That boy isn't up to a whole bunch. Acts like an honest day's work might kill him. Ever meet his mother? A sad case. Has been since she lost her older boy. He was the apple of her eye. Maybe that's why Greg's how he is. He and Michael were real close. Well, I'd best be getting back to the business. Come again soon."

Come again soon.

What alternative did I have? The Co-op offered the lowest prices and the biggest selection, and I was obliged to shop there and suffer Wally Gossip's nosy presence. Eventually, with more cash in the kitty, I could reduce my Co-op visits by obtaining merchandise in larger quantities: six cases of motor oil, ten saw blades, whatever. Limiting my trips to the Co-op, and the rest of the world past the front gate, was, I theorized, necessary for my personal transformation. People passing through my life tended to implant distracting, totally worthless thoughts. (Was Sonia a lesbian? Why should I find myself speculating, even momentarily, about a store clerk's sexual leanings?) Restricting my contact with conventional society would strengthen my relationship with Jessie, the most compassionate, positive-minded woman on earth, and Alex, the child I hadn't spent enough time nurturing. Perhaps that was the reason Greg rarely ventured outside the Dunes — he was tightening his bonds with Susan — but I strongly suspected it wasn't. His behaviour implied he was governed by a more complex, and evidently more painful, purpose. He appeared to be terrified of strangers.

We were at Mirror Lake one summer afternoon when a car cruising the normally deserted road, halted, reversed, and slipped into the clearing close behind us. Greg scrambled erect and scurried bare foot into the bush. The interloper, a young woman, sat in her car for a while devouring potato chips and admiring the glinting lake. After she drove off, Greg emerged from hiding and, without an explanation, resettled on his beach towel. In his own home, strangers wheeling into the yard caused Greg to whip upstairs, mutely assigning Susan to deal with them. From my perspective, running away was not, in itself, an exceptionally peculiar act. That was, after all, how I ended up in northern Alberta. But Greg's anguished countenance, and the sudden haste of his move to safety were extremely odd. If he wasn't a criminal fugitive — and as lots of Preston residents knew where he lived, I was certain he wasn't — then he was plagued by a

back
roads
Ted
Ferguson

strange and mighty force, a psychological beast that I wished I could slay for him.

] Two days after we made it home from the Co-op, a savage blizzard pitched across the stubbled farmlands and up into the hills. It was engrossing to watch wind and snow hammer the submissive valley surrounding our house as though it were levelling a gigantic sheet of warped tin. Then the storm retreated and a ribbon of blue air enlivened the southern brim of the overcast sky. Encased in ski jackets and felt-lined boots, we trooped outside. The air was cold and pure and strikingly still. We shovelled paths to the coal pile and the deadwood stack, and we gathered snow in canners to melt on the stove for wash water.

Tying shovels to a sled, we trudged to the gate. There was no urgency involved — we weren't travelling anywhere — but Alex claimed digging the truck out was a priority, for it didn't like being smothered any more than we would. As children tend to do, he attributed human characteristics to the Black Bobcat: cranky (often hesitant to start), playful (the seat bounced going over pot-holes), and bravely unfashionable (a shabbily dressed ugly duckling). On the road to the gate, snow snuggled the ankles of fenceposts and trees and burdened the spines of overhanging branches. There were no birds and no animal tracks; the owl was in its nest. The silence was thick and invincible; the sound of our voices barely scratched it.

While Jessie and Alex cleared the snow off the truck, I assessed the storm's impact on the municipal road. The builders had, thank goodness, left the charming, tree-shaded old road from the highway undisturbed, concentrating on the trail-like route that lay between the road and the ravine near the end of our property line. The new addition was straight and smooth and banked on both sides. Gazing at curvy snow drifts, I wondered if the plow would unclog the road later that day or sometime the following morning.

It did neither. More snow — steady, windless downfalls — came overnight and the next afternoon, and the plow operator, waiting for a clear-sky forecast, stranded us for three days. Alex was pleased. He hauled out the games I never played with him in Vancouver: Battleship, Masterpiece, and a gruesome creation in which poor Miss Peach was walloped to death in the library with a monkey wrench.

On truly hideous days, with fifty-below temperatures shutting the Sunnyside school, we played close to the self-feeder stove, dampening the coal lumps to make them burn more slowly — Greg's remedy for my having trucked in an inadequate supply. On some truly splendid days, the temperature up, the sky a vibrant blue, Jessie drove me to the Greyhound bus stop at the Preston Mall, where I'd ride off to Prairie locales to conduct interviews for magazine articles.

We had few visitors: Frank once or twice a week; Susan and Greg far less often. A duo of parka-clad youths conveyed the *Book of Mormon* to our door, and, equally as unsuccessful, an enthusiastic woman in an Edmonton Oilers toque and matching scarf attempted to sell us Amway toilet bowl cleanser, even though we had an outhouse. The half-mile walk, a short distance to us, constituted a challenge of marathon proportions to most people. The motor vehicle had ruined the notion of foot power in rural communities like it did everywhere else. In Preston, it was said, only retirees and welfare cases walked. Many residents drove back and forth on Palliser, rejecting excellent spaces, in order to park within steps of their destination. A shop owner who lived two blocks from his business drove to and from work.

One sunny morning, at the tail end of March, I was shovelling snow off the roof when a blurry figure snagged the corner of my eye. A stranger was descending the hill: a slow-moving, square-bodied man attired in a tweed cap and a long, wool overcoat. He was clutching a dark-covered book. Who was it this time, I growled to myself, a Jehovah's Witness?

The stranger raised his hand in a cordial greeting. Straddling the porch peak, I nodded. He came to the foot of the ladder.

"Whooee, that's a helluva a hike. Gotta be days you wanna hug the fire till spring."

"Definitely. What can I do for you?"

"A little conversation, that's all. A little conversation." He peered at the porch door, hinting, I thought, that I ought to be good neighbourly and invite him inside for a cup of coffee. I let the hint glide past me. Jessie was waxing the floors and I was reluctant to interrupt her, especially if the stranger was a Bible-pusher we would have to prod back through the door. "Briggs's my name. Clayton Briggs. I've a spread at Simpson's Landing."

"How can I help you, Mr. Briggs?"

"You mind coming down? I don't hear good. Left ear's half deaf, the other's headin' south." I climbed down the ladder. "You folks must be lonely. Not a blessed soul for miles. I brung this for the wife. I got a slew of them at an auction. It's hers for keeps." He placed the book in my hand. It was bound in dark green leather, low-grade Moroccan. I opened the book to the title page. *Reckless Hearts*. A romance novel.

"Thank you."

"You ever met my brother Pete?"

"No, I don't think so."

"This was his quarter. He grazed horses on it. A lame excuse for a road followed the fenceline. I see you hacked it again. Anyhow, Pete didn't pay the taxes. Ten years, not a red penny. I'd have lent him the dough but he's got grass for brains — he didn't say squat till the municipal district seized the quarter and you folks nabbed it. The thing is, I'd like it in the family again. I'll give you a decent price, five hundred more than what you paid, plus extra for the building."

"I'm sorry. I can't do that."

"Can't or don't fancy to?"

"Don't fancy to. This is our home."

"It's a mystery to me why you'd wanna have a home in a place with no neighbours. Your boy's gotta be miserable. No kids to play with."

"He loves it here."

"Tell you what. I'll jack the price up two-fifty."

"Sorry. I'm not selling."

"Okay. You change your tune, I'm in the phone book. Clayton Briggs. Simpson's Landing." He smiled slightly and, as though he was speaking to himself, he muttered, "Doesn't that beat all."

"Pardon me?"

"I was thinking how this isn't what I expected. I waited till winter was nearly done. I reckoned you'd have had your fill of cold and snow. You gotta be born hereabouts to have the gumption to stay. City folk, they aren't up to snuff. No offence, but by and large your kind of people are spoiled weaklings."

The witcher was Frank's idea. A plumber by trade, he had been dousing for thirty years, maintaining records of underground streams within a fifty-mile radius of his farm. "He'll land you a well, and a deep one," Frank said. "His dad was a witcher and his dad's dad. It's in his blood."

5 The witcher wheeled into our yard on a cool, spring morning, scramble-haired and unshaven, wearing a plaid shirt and baggy corduroys. The green-lettered words "Shamrock Plumbing" were inscribed on the panel of his van, above the image of a goofy-faced leprechaun grasping a bathroom plunger. He took a short, metal rod off the front seat and, proceeding to the rear of the van, pulled out a case of beer.

"Oh, no," Jessie murmured. "He's a boozer."

I heard a clinking sound as he walked to the spot where we waited, at the edge of the slender, windbreak treeline lying between the house and the field. The case was jammed with bottles, and I was relieved to realize that he wasn't anticipating drinking himself into an unreliable fog; the top of the case was missing, and the bottles were old and empty.

"I understand you're a wordsmith," he said. "Do you write novels?"

"No, journalism."

"Journalism is literature in a hurry."

"That's a clever description."

"It isn't mine. Matthew Arnold's. You must do a fair amount of reading. I'm halfway through *The Red and the Black* at the moment. How do you rate John Fowles? *The Magus* was a strenuous read but I enjoyed it. Are you a fan of Fowles' writing?"

"I haven't tried him." I hadn't tried Stendhal either. The grubby, well-witching plumber was better read than I was.

"Where should I start?"

"Right here," Jessie said. "Or somewhere else in the vicinity of the house."

The witcher fingered his spiky chin. "I'll do my best, madam, but water's unpredictable. That lake doesn't mean anything. Every inch of your property might be bone-dry. Am I alarming you? Forgive me. I wasn't aiming to. For all I know, we're standing on a subterranean river. Go six feet and you'll hit it. Like I said, water's unpredictable."

For a two and half hours he circled the building, dipping and lifting the metal rod, arranging bottles in intersecting lines, transferring them once he detected another, stronger possibility. Focusing on his mission, he suspended conversation until he rested, which he frequently did, and was smoking cigarettes and staring at the latest configuration of bottles as if one of them might suddenly upend itself, the neck pointing to water below it. He spoke of his background. Despite the company's name and the silly leprechaun, he wasn't Irish. He was a German immigrant whose English was impressively accent-free. He took over the plumbing company after quitting his original profession, teaching high school. "The business is known all over the countryside as Shamrock Plumbing. I'd be an idiot to scrap the name. Canadians love the familiar and hate the unknown. And what would I change it to? 'Frankfurt am Main Plumbing'? With a picture of a smiley frankfurter diving into a plugged drain? No, sir. No way."

Why did he quit teaching?

"Kids today don't respect their teachers. They're smart-alecky. They don't study. They fall asleep in class. A teacher punishes a student, and the parents scream at the principal. The principal's petrified of being sued for cruelty to a minor, so he screams at the teacher. I don't get any of that in plumbing. I'm my own boss. No one to answer to. I fix your pipes, you're grateful. To the general public, teaching's a noble occupation and plumbing isn't, but the truth is, plumbing beats teaching by a country mile."

Jessie missed the witcher's comments on his former profession. She was baking chocolate chip cookies. He was pausing and grabbing for a cigarette package when she swept out of the house bearing a serving platter. Postponing his smoke, the witcher plucked a

back
roads
Ted
Ferguson

cookie off the platter, stuck the whole thing in his mouth, chewed vigorously, and swallowed it in jumbled sections. He thanked my wife while stowing two cookies in his shirt pocket. "Childhood revisited," he said. "I'm saving these for after lunch. Cookies and a glass of milk. I'll be a kid again."

"Speaking of lunch," Jessie said, "would you like to eat with us?"

"I won't be here."

"Will you be coming tomorrow morning?" I asked. "We'll make sure we're home."

"No need to come. I've found water."

"Water?" I blurted. "Why didn't you tell me?"

Disregarding my question, he said, "It's under the rock."

"What rock?"

"The flat one in front of you. It isn't on the side of the house you wanted, but it's within spitting distance of the rear wall, and you won't have to carry it very far."

"How deep will we have to dig?" Jessie inquired.

"I wish I knew. Dousing isn't precise. It doesn't include a built-in tape measure. But I do have a hunch you'll be lucky. Ten feet. Twelve. And don't worry, you'll have a generous supply that won't run dry."

That was exciting news. A good well, next to the house. All I had to do was dig. In contrast to making the fenceline road, that appeared to be about as arduous as scraping and varnishing a coffee table. Moulding the road was an artistic endeavour: bush sculpture. The result was as enthralling, in my biased opinion, as some of the works I'd pondered in city exhibitions, such as the pyramid of cemented pebbles I saw in a Toronto gallery. Urging water from the ground was a creative act, but there wouldn't be a speck of beauty in it, only the chest-swelling pleasure of realizing that, like the pioneers, I did it myself.

The witcher lit a cigarette, climbed in his van and headed up the road.

I pushed a shovel into the soil and began digging the dirt surrounding the rock. It wasn't the smooth start I hoped for. What looked like a small, flat rock on the surface was, beneath the earth, a long, thick, jagged boulder. Jessie and I tried to extract it. We strained and sweated, and although it stirred slightly, we lacked the physical power to force it up from its socket. Frank arrived while the dinner roast was cooking and, using a crowbar and a two-by-four, he helped me leverage the boulder out.

For the next couple of days, everything was hunky-dory. I dug a knee-deep hole, wide enough to stand in and fling dirt. And then, at the four-foot level, the Devil noticed what I was doing and, remembering I mocked him at a screening of the *Exorcist*, he sought revenge. A carpet of blue clay covered the bottom of the hole. How deep did the vein run? Was a vast motherlode of the hellish stuff lying below my feet?

The clay defied normal digging. Each time I placed my foot on the top of the shovel blade I had to push extremely hard to peel off a fraction of an inch. By the end of the fifth day, I was tired and frustrated and fighting the idea of hiring a professional driller. Obstinacy compelled me to dig; obstinacy and the belief that I'd feel like a puny-willed fool, and a money-wasting fool at that, if the drill went two inches and hit water. I struggled on and nine days after the clay appeared I defeated Satan, striking dirt.

Thank goodness, I thought, tossing a shovel load to the surface, I haven't much further to dig.

back
roads
Ted
Ferguson

6

Frank carried a photograph of his wife in his wallet. A sepia snapshot, Scotch tape repairing a bad tear, showing a woman in her mid-twenties seated on a dog sled, a parka and a Hudson's Bay blanket defending her body against winter abuse. Judith had once worked someplace beyond nowhere, a territory of trappers and hunters and prospectors, huskies, snowshoes, and cross-country skis. An outpost resident took the picture with a Brownie. The old photograph was proof of Frank's big catch, evidence that Judith was "a stunner who turned young men to jelly." In her sixties, she wasn't a stunner anymore, but the dramatic, midnight-black hair endured, still trimmed in a pageboy, and the dark eyes, warm and wide and trusting, were now cool and wary and imbued with hard-knocks wisdom. She was a handsome woman who, if social conditioning hadn't trained them to believe aging was repugnant, may have still turned young men to jelly.

"Why haven't we crossed paths before today?" Judith asked, soliciting my attention with her large, cautious eyes. "You've been here since last summer."

"It's weird. We just missed you twice when you were at your son's."

"My husband tells me your first winter was a shock to the system."

"January was the biggest shock. Some mornings there was frost on the wall beside Alex's bed. But we survived to tell the tale. Even poor Alex, sleeping with his clothes on."

"I don't wish to discourage you, but it can get much worse. That was a mild winter. One week of fifty-below weather and not a great deal of snow. Wait until it's fifty-below for weeks on end, and you're saying this cold spell can't last, and it does. And snow. We've had enormous storms here, drifts over your head. It takes the municipal crews weeks to open outlying roads. Weeks."

Susan had scrounged a picnic table somewhere — another breast-fancier's tribute, I assumed — and we were lounging on the seats, sipping rose hip tea in flowing sunlight. The atmosphere was curiously reserved. The generally busy-mouthed Frank gnawed at the edges of the conversation, agreeing with whatever his wife said, while Susan and Greg were clearly ill-at-ease. All three of them were deferring to Judith. With her silk scarf, freshly laundered pants suit, and rigid carriage, she was visiting royalty, a backwoods queen.

"I don't mind being cut off from civilization," Jessie said. "I can read all day."

"My father was a tremendous reader," Judith said. "He had an extensive book collection. It's at the lodge. Would you like to see it? Frank will show you."

"Sure. I can always use something to read."

"No, no," Judith said sternly. "The books belong in the lodge. They are not to be borrowed."

"You want to go?" Frank said. "It's down the trail over there."

Not interested in pursuing books she was forbidden to read, Jessie replied politely, "No, thank you. Some other time."

I said I'd go. I felt like walking and I was inquisitive; no one had ever mentioned there was a lodge on the property. Jessie asked me to check on Alex first. He was last spotted ducking into the barn, bearing the irrational faith that the pregnant cat would deliver kittens the second he walked in. The cat, its belly crowded, was sleeping on a bale of straw. Alex was gone, an indication that he was either in the chicken pen, flapping his arms and crowing to confuse the confusion-prone birds, or chasing Susan and Greg's cow around the pasture, trying to climb onto its back.

He was in the pen.

"Are we getting chickens?"

"No. Your mother hates them. She thinks they're brainless."

"I'll look after them. She won't have to buy eggs."

"No chickens."

Susan had Kool Aid for Alex. He gulped half a glass, and, praying she would contradict my unsatisfactory reaction, he implored his mother to let him have chickens.

"Only if they're dead and stuffed," she said, "and you promise not to bring them to the kitchen table."

Strolling to the path, Frank and I passed Judith's maroon Chrysler. Judith suffered from an unexplained health problem, frequently confining herself to her bed for weeks at a time, and, under-employed, the Chrysler was an immaculate chunk of machinery, inside and out, a respectable sight in a town where respectability was a rule written in stone.

On the trail, a weed-congested slit in the woods, I told Frank my father-in-law said chickens were eternally pecking at the ground because they were trying to dig up some common sense.

"He pegged that right. When I was a boy, my neighbour had a pet chicken. It hadn't a molecule of common sense. None whatsoever. It stood and gaped at the sky in rain storms. It was pouring one day and the blasted bird was staring with its mouth wide open and damned if it didn't swallow so much water it drowned itself. The honest truth. It drowned itself. Know what you should get? Goats."

"Goats?"

"Don't be that way."

"What way?"

"Like I'm suggesting something putrid. Goats don't warrant their bad name. They're intelligent. And clean. Drop food in the dirt and they won't eat it. And there's money in them. Breed goats and farmers will snap the kids up. Owing to the shortage. A nice sideline for you and Jessie."

"Why is there a shortage?"

"The organic trade. Goat cheese is a hot seller in the city. Goat farms are rare and they can't keep pace with the demand. Goats are ideal for you folks. I've tasted the milk and it's fine. Healthier than the homogenized crap in grocery stores."

The lodge was at the end of the trail. Tucked amid poplars on the lip of a deserted lake, it was a low, unadorned structure with paint-desperate walls and moss nibbling on selected roof shingles. In contrast, the interior was washed, waxed, and vacuumed, surprisingly well-tended for an empty nest. A rocker and a Mission chair rested on a faded Persian rug, confronting an oak armoire and an oil painting of a wader-clad angler casting his line in a sleepy river. A Brier-filled pipe rack and an ivory chess set stood on a round, oak table. The dead businessman's presence hung in the air like bluntly spoken words. Maybe maintaining her father's aura as if he was a literary colossus or a political figure worthy of enshrinement brought light to a dark space in Judith's heart, but, personally, I thought the room was creepy. Keeping my sentiments to myself, I scanned the floor-to-ceiling bookcase. The mysteries (Wilkie Collins, Conan Doyle, S.S. Van Dine) and the books on religion and philosophy were of limited appeal, but there were first-class novels (*Sister Carrie, Vandover and the Brute*) and a book I was tempted to smuggle out under my shirt, *The Voyage of the Beagle.*

"The books been dusted?" Frank asked.

"Dusted? Yes, I think so. On the lower shelves anyway."

"Judith's upset if Susan skips the books."

"Susan cleans this place?"

"Twice a week."

"She does a terrific job."

"She'd better. Judith won't pay her for being sloppy."

The lodge was built by a group of middle-management types from the city. In the autumn, they travelled north, got drunk, and shot ducks. When they ultimately wearied of drinking and killing, or maybe of each other, they put the building on the market. Judith's father wasn't drawn to liquor or shooting ducks; he obtained the lodge for the solitude. A widower, he retreated to it whenever he felt the pull to escape Preston. He read, listened to marching bands and Viennese waltzes, and roamed the adjoining Crown land photographing plants and wildlife.

"Her dad cast a giant shadow over Judith," Frank revealed. "She had boyfriends, but none held a candle to him. Daddy's girl, even after he passed away. The fact of the matter is, she loved a memory more than she loved anybody she dated."

The room was influencing Frank. Reviving ghosts, turning him reflective. I knew hardly anything about Judith and now that I'd finally met her and witnessed her repressive effect on family members, I was immensely curious. Dining at our house, Frank lavished words on the latest news stories and regional events, and he often repeated godawful jokes he heard on the Preston station's popular feature, *The Noonday Knee-Slapper*. If he referred to his family, it was to impart inconsequential knowledge: he was giving his wife an electric kettle for her birthday; Greg triggered throbbing sinus headaches eating ice cream. "Judith's an attractive woman," I said.

"That might not be a hundred percent so, what I just said. She did love someone a lot, maybe as passionately as she loved her dad. He was a medical doctor. They had an affair lasting years and years. She would've followed him to the moon, but he wasn't that hot on her."

"He jilted her."

"In the worst way."

"A note in her mailbox."

"Worse. He had his new girl tell her. Judith's best friend. Judith fell to pieces. Crying night and day. And that's when I met her. I was working at Esso and I fixed her transmission. Straight off the bat, I was dying to marry her. We dated a month and then I proposed. She wanted to talk to her dad before saying yes or no. He was a kindly sort, Tom Graham. He was leery of her marrying on the rebound from a heart-breaking affair, but he said, 'If you think Frank Tyson can make you happy, go ahead and do it.' Judith had plans for me rising above mechanics. Her dad hired me to run a business of his, but I didn't have it in me to laze at a desk and give orders. Yet, after all's said and done, the marriage worked fine. Judith's an emotional lady, easily hurt. I only went to grade eight and I don't know much about a whole bunch of things, but I do know how to take care of Judith."

When we returned to the house, Judith was sitting in the Chrysler, looking sullen and detached, locked in an impenetrable room. Frank went to her, looking sympathetic and oddly rejuvenated, thankful to be needed. Jessie and Susan were at the picnic table, by themselves, awash in domestic chatter.

"Broccoli spaghetti?" Susan was saying. "You're doing a number on me."

"No, really, it's delicious. Fry broccoli with mushrooms and garlic, then blend it with the pasta in a mixing bowl. Ted thrives on it, and he normally won't eat broccoli. Isn't that right, darling?"

I nodded and smiled and contemplated the amazing truth that two vastly contradictory women had settled comfortably in my wife's mind. The intellectual Jessie, a former art student with a preference for the French Impressionists, Dante and T.S. Eliot, piano concertos and left-wing politics, and the homemaker Jessie, the splendid cook, adept seamstress, and household barber. The complex shadings of the progeny of a difficult Ukrainian father and a sweet-natured Scottish mother.

"Did you try my recipe?" Susan asked. "The carrot muffins?"

"Not yet. I will soon." Alex came out of the barn and walked towards the table. The Chrysler cruised past us. Frank elevated a hand in a good-bye gesture, but Judith declined to acknowledge we were anything but particles of air, and contaminated air at that.

"Where's Greg?" Susan called.

Alex shrugged. "Dunno. He wasn't with me."

"On his own again," Susan said. "His privacy's so important to him. Sure you guys won't stay for supper?"

"I'm sure," Jessie said. "Ted wants to do more digging."

Alex rode home in the back of the truck, against the cab, offering himself to wind and sun.

"How was the lodge?"

"Bizarre. The place is exactly as her father left it. His smoking jacket's in the closet. She must have had it dry-cleaned recently. It's in the plastic bag. Judith pays Susan to clean the lodge. Everything's so spic and span she probably washes the mice too. What happened with Greg's mother? She seemed pretty grim."

"I wish I knew. Susan was saying she found a fabulous winter coat at the Goodwill, and for some mysterious reason Judith took offence, jumped up, and marched to the car. It wasn't the first time. Susan says sudden exits are her specialty."

"Same as Greg."

"It isn't the same. Greg runs from people; Judith reacts to things people say. Those long periods she spends in bed — I think she's depressed."

"It's possible. Whether she's depressed or not, she's hard to take. Extremely self-centred."

"Like mother, like son."

"She talked to us and asked questions, but I could tell she really wasn't interested in a word we said."

Jessie glanced through the window behind us. Alex was obeying her instructions; he wasn't standing up and he wasn't leaning over the side to watch the tires throw gravel. "He's alright." She swung her head around, studied the road momentarily, and then issued her final verdict on Greg's touchy mother. "Judith's suffering. She lost her son. Anyone who hasn't lost a child hasn't the right to judge the actions of someone who has."

Push, lift, fill the bucket.

Over and over, hour upon hour.

Damp spots dotted the walls and there was a trickle that lasted a day, but not a drop of water materialized at the bottom of the hole, not after four feet, not after six, not at the eight-foot mark. Nevertheless, I clung to my optimism, although the grip was gradually loosening. The witcher had declared that dousing was an imprecise system, but he was certain I would find water under the rock. More perseverance was required, the spirit of a marathoner.

"Maybe you should hire Frank's friend to help you dig," Jessie proposed during breakfast.

"Why?"

"It will go faster."

"He isn't Frank's friend. He rents a house from Judith and Frank collects the money."

"He isn't logging this summer. He's restless. He's sick of hanging around the house."

"I'm not hiring anybody. I want to do it myself. I've already told you that."

"It's your decision, but if it was me, I'd be glad to get some assistance."

It was a splendid day for digging. Cool air, chubby, white clouds furnishing a teal blue sky. I retrieved the shovel, went to the well site and yanked the plastic covering aside. The well had shed its disguise overnight. What I had accepted at face value to be a harmless entity was, in reality, untrustworthy and highly dangerous. Part of a wall had collapsed, heaping dirt on the floor. I was shocked, not only by the chance that the whole well could've caved in while I was digging, burying me alive, but by my own stupidity, the fact that it never occurred to me to shore up the walls. The partial collapse was a warning, and I took it to heart.

back
roads
Ted
Ferguson

Jessie was on the porch, hunting for her gloves, the prelude to a tiring session of dragging the dirt bucket to the surface. She smiled and said lightly, "That it, you finished for the day?"

"Actually, I am. That man Frank knows, I think I'll hire him."

The logger came bearing the signia of his occupation. A chainsaw scar blemished his cheek. His wrists were too thick for a watch and his shirts, extra large, were as tight as a second skin on his chest and shoulders. He was, he said, so big that if the saw sliced off half of his body there would be enough left over for him to go on logging. His size made an impact wherever he went, impressing or intimidating, and, perhaps because it spoke for him, he didn't talk much. When he did, his voice was a whispery purr, his views positive and non-judgmental.

Well-digging ran in his family: his grandfather dug wells, his father dug wells, his brother dug wells. For themselves, neighbours, and friends in poverty-humbled rural Ontario settings. He himself acquired ten acres of barren ground in Perth County, set a dilapidated trailer on it, and shovelled for water. He made no effort to locate a witcher. Choosing a spot at random, he dug a hole and, finding no water, filled it in again. On his fourth hole he hit a stream. His well-digging experience included the making of wall cribbing. For our well he measured the pit, cut fir boards, and nailed them together in a solid, four-foot-long square. He built the cribbing next to the well. Upon completion, he fell to his knees, grasped the framework, and with an astounding burst of physical power, upended it into the hole. "That wasn't so horrible, was it?" he said, unscrewing his thermos top. "I'll sit on my rump awhile and drink coffee and then I'll do the next section."

I took a break too. I joined Jessie in the living room. She was reclining on the couch, reading John le Carré.

"How's it going?"

"That guy's incredible. The cribbing must have weighed a hundred pounds. He picked it up and dropped it into the well."

"I hope his bill won't be incredible. Has he said yet what he's charging us?"

"No. I asked him again this morning. He didn't answer. He went on unloading the two by fours from his truck. So I said, 'I'm concerned that we can't afford you. Lumberjacks earn big wages.' 'Don't sweat it,' was all he said, 'I won't ding you an arm and a leg.'"

"Whatever it is, it'll be worth it. We couldn't build the cribbing by ourselves."

"Of course, we could. We couldn't have moved it, but we could've built it."

Taking turns in the pit, the logger and I passed the twelve-foot level. There were rocks and a second petering-out trickle, but no abundant water source. The logger told me digging stories, of well-seekers uncovering arrowheads and dinosaur bones, a baby's skull, an Evinrude engine, and a rubber boot stuffed with Canadian Tire dollars. On the day we reached fifteen feet he climbed the ladder, opened his thermos, and told me something I was reluctant to hear. "I'm not in the habit of questioning another man's ways," he said, "but things can drag on and maybe they shouldn't. Sometimes a man's obliged to step back and think long and hard and maybe change his course."

"The well — is that what you're saying? I ought to quit digging?"

"It's up to you, but me, I wouldn't go no farther."

Neither would I. Not now, not after he had spoken up, giving voice to thoughts I had been rejecting for weeks. An obstinate little bugger, I would have shovelled to the centre of the earth, clutching my pallid optimism like a battle-worn flag, until someone said what begged to be said and I felt compelled to accept the truth, to suffer the sad, savage cut of disappointment. I was free, of course, to summon the witcher and target a new venue. But what if he was on a losing streak? What if I dug a second hole — or a third or a fourth — and all of them were desert dry? Obstinacy yielded the house and the fenceline road, but obstinacy wasn't always rewarded. Louis Riel failed, and so did Ed Wood, and unless she's just taking her time crossing the Pacific, so did Amelia Earhart. Defeat was part of the contract, the agreement everyone signed upon birth, and the fifteen-foot hole wasn't likely to be my last failure.

"It is time to quit, isn't it? I wish I'd done it sooner. Now I've got this huge hole in my yard. Fifteen feet of useless space."

"There's got to be some purpose for it."

"A missile silo. A garbage dump. A PCB storage container."

The logger finished his coffee, extracted the ladder from the pit and covered the opening with boards. Someday, I'd shovel the dirt back in the pit. Someday, when it didn't distress me to go near it.

"So where we digging next?" the logger asked.

"Nowhere. I'll have somebody drill it. We should settle up before you leave. How much do I owe you?"

"Nothing."

"That's impossible," I said, taken aback.

"When I like a man, I don't take his money."

"But you have to. You deserve to be paid. You worked hard."

"That wasn't work, that was exercise. Staying in shape for camp. I draw top wages logging. You're a family man and you're obviously not rich, so you can use the cash more than me."

"But you deserve to be paid," I repeated.

"Tell you what. Come the weekend, we'll barbecue steaks. You buy them, and the VO, and providing you don't hog the bottle, we'll shake hands and call us even."

The drill truck owner wasn't so generous: one hundred dollars a foot, cash, no cheque, no credit card. Two hundred and fifty bucks before he switched the engine on, the rest the minute he packed it in, dry hole or wet. He had been burned many times, his demeanour declared, and gazing at me, a scruffy bush creature, he saw the threat of more damaging flames.

I forked over the engine-initiating fee. Cash, no cheque, no credit card. Fine and dandy, he said. How deep do I drill if water doesn't show? Sixteen hundred dollars' deep, I apprised him. That, I added, would deflate my well fund and I'd have to save money and contact him again in the fall.

I pointed to the foot of the field, to a flat strip directly in line with the kitchen. Why there? he frowned. Why not nearer the house? It was level with the lake, I said. It seemed logical that if the lake was feeding subterranean channels they'd be situated at the base of the sloping field, not on the plateau where the house stood. You're the boss, the driller said, but I recollect my grand-dad digging ten yards from a lake and he came up dry. You know what's best for you? Get a witcher.

Jessie was in town with Susan. Shopping and filling the five-gallon containers. The driller had arrived hours behind schedule, and Alex was due home. I hopped in the Black Bobcat, wheeled to the gate and, turning the truck around, sat waiting, twitchy as hell, wondering whether our homesteading dreams were liable to be wrecked by the absence of water anywhere on the quarter. I was dying to witness the drilling but I couldn't let Alex walk down our road alone, fearful of engendering a *Preston Gazette* headline, "Local Man Watches Drilling While Bear Snacks On Son." Finally, more than an hour late, the van transporting Alex from a children's group outing glided into sight.

I hustled Alex into the truck and drove to the field.

"You've got water," the driller proclaimed as I slid out of the Chevy.

"Fantastic," I said, relief rolling over me.

Sixteen feet.

"Terrific."

"You're one lucky sonovabitch. Wells don't always come that easy."

back
roads
Ted
Ferguson

{63}

Brother Henri was laughing. Standing beside his truck, he was looking down at the plastic sheet covering my coal pile remnants — mostly flaky lumps and black dust — and behaving as though he was viewing a television sitcom. I grinned, figuring whatever was amusing him called for a grin, but I really didn't understand why he was acting that way. Was plastic a funny object to him, or did Brother Henri and the Servants of the Adored Blood, feeling elevated to a superior level, laugh at everything they encountered in the nonsensical society surrounding the coal yard?

"Plastic," he said, the laughter declining. "Boy, oh boy, that's a good one."

"Is it really?"

"Plastic's transparent. Light shines through and destroys the coal. Makes it crumble faster. Coal likes darkness. Coal likes basements."

"I don't have a basement."

"Leave it to me. I'll fix you up."

"With a basement?"

"This old tarpaulin's in my shed. I'm delivering to Sunnyside next week and I'll scoot up from the highway and leave it inside your gate."

"Great."

Brother Henri stripped the plastic sheet off, crawled into the truck cab, and, maneouvering into position, dumped a ton of coal on the disintegrating remains. When he hopped from the cab, holding his receipt book, I invited him into the house for coffee.

"Sorry, my friend. Today's Tuesday and coffee can't pass my lips."

"Why's that?"

"The denial of self-indulgence. Moral strength through physical adversity. We shun coffee on Mondays, Tuesdays, and Wednesdays."

"Is coffee the only self-indulgence you deny yourselves?"

"We don't smoke on Thursdays, Fridays, and Saturdays."

"How about Sunday?"

"No smoking and no coffee, but we don't mind because we're too busy to notice. Sunday's our day for sex."

"You and the nuns?"

He assessed my expression and burst into laughter. "I'm pulling your leg. Boy, did you ever fall for it. 'You and the nuns?' Hilarious." I paid the bill and he scribbled a receipt. "That's how people in these parts think. Henri and his ladies, wild orgies. Well, their thinking's silly. Me and the Sisters are celibate. Purity's a rung on the ladder to Heaven."

With its anti-Vatican and no-nooky policies, I imagined the Servants of the Adored Blood had trouble recruiting members. On the contrary, Brother Henri said. Disgruntled women were forever writing letters and, on occasion, journeying to the coal yard to plead their case for enrolment. Lacking space to accommodate additional Sisters, Brother Henri included the coal industry in his prayers, soliciting its revival as a household fuel source, thereby enabling the company to construct a larger residence.

"Tough slogging, the coal business. We've got food and a roof over our heads, but it's a struggle to break even. Praise God, the Sisters are beavers. Work, work, work. Don't complain. Don't say forget coal, let's open a doughnut shop in the West Edmonton Mall. Most were with me in Quebec. They didn't want to live there after the stink in the newspapers. Did you hear of it?"

"No."

"The police raided us. They put me away."

Clearly, they didn't put him away soon enough.

Prior to founding his religious order, Brother Henri wrote and distributed pamphlets criticizing Papal leniency, and he personally harassed Montreal diocese officials. He advocated empowering priests to publicly denounce marital cheaters and corrupt politicians by name. Above all else, he aspired to change the educational system. To banish sports and music programs and swamp grade school classrooms in religious awareness. Ten Hail Marys plus four Hail Marys equals fourteen Hail Marys. A is for Adam, B is for Bible, C is for Confession. Somehow, Brother Henri laid his hands on a mini-bus crammed with small children. He drove the vehicle to a country house. The bottom floor was converted into a classroom; the second floor a dormitory. He and his female companions were bent on detaining and educating the children for a school term to show the church how superior their teaching methods were. Within hours, the dream died. The police swooped in and arrested them. "I did it wrong. I should've asked the parents for permission to borrow their children."

"I can't see any parent lending his kid to you."

"I can. There are strange people in this world."

"Oh, yes, definitely."

"Now you know Brother Henri's story. Now you know why I'm not in Quebec. The press vilified me. I felt out of place. I just didn't fit in anymore."

] A misfit.

Tramping west in pursuit of a new life.

That was a repetitive theme in the province's early history. Contemporary authors and historians prefer describing pioneering settlers as gutsy adventurers or bright-brained visionaries, which many of them may have been, but Alberta was also a collection bin for freaks and lunatics, crooks and fanatics, the disgraced and the disillusioned, the brazen and the shy. Misfits of every class and character.

The Barr expedition was tailor-sewn for the socially flawed. In 1903, nineteen hundred shopkeepers, factory hands, waiters, and assorted Britons fed up with their lives migrated to the Canadian West under the leadership of Anglican minister I.M. Barr. The colonists intended to rough it in the bush, farming raw land, but their perception of roughing it differed from most settlers. They jammed thirty boxcars with personal possessions; some people were so ill-informed about frontier existence they packed electric lamps, pianos, and pith helmets. The colonists bungled and learned, endured and succeeded. (One ever-lasting mistake was establishing a community, Lloydminster, on the fourth meridian — the Alberta-Saskatchewan boundary line divided the settlement in half.)

Francis Dickens also bungled, learned, and endured, but he didn't succeed. Fleeing the shadow of his celebrated father, Charles, he joined the North-West Mounted Police in 1874. In the old country Francis, a stuttering, partially deaf sleepwalker, felt like an outsider, uncomfortable wherever he was. He dropped out of medical school and failed to attain a Foreign Office posting. Entering the NWMP at the rank of inspector, he garnered a reputation during twelve years of service as being a lazy, alcoholic, inept loner. Owing to either bad horsemanship or good whisky, he embarrassed himself by falling off his mount leading a charge against rifle-firing Blackfoot.

Dickens at least earned his own way in the New World. That wasn't the case for many of his fellow countrymen, the so-called "remittance men." Unable to adapt to unbendable rules imposed by English society, they were paid by their affluent families to avoid their native land. Determined to convince themselves that cashing remittance cheques wasn't their only skill, some well-bred undesirables took up beekeeping and amateur acting while others, harbouring no ambition to establish their worthiness, made themselves at home in saloon chairs and brothel beds. A countless number of remittance men lived out their cowboy fantasies, signing on as ranch hands. The abundance of remittance men and other British expatriates in cattle-country during the late 1800s led to the formation of a sports league that, considering its frontier milieu, was almost bizarre — it was comprised of polo teams.

Train robbers, whisky traders, card sharks, and hookers — misfits by anybody's definition — rooted in the province. Harry Longbaugh, a.k.a. the Sundance Kid, was a ranch hand near High River. Thumbing his nose at a city ordinance, freed South Carolina slave John Ware drove a herd through the streets of Calgary en route to his homestead. Noted oddball Smoky Lee repelled Blackfoot attackers and scribbled in his diary, "Not much to say today. Got 2 Buffalo, ate Prairie Chicken, killed 3 Blackfoot." A fellow eccentric, Harry (Kanouse) Taylor, posted a sign in the lobby of his Fort Macleod hotel that read, "Guests are expected to rise at 6:00 AM as the sheets are needed for tablecloths."

The Canadian West's greatest frontiersman, John George (Kootenai) Brown, crossed the ocean upon deciding that he and the British Army were miserably mismatched. The Irish-born Brown was serving in India, where he allegedly killed an officer in a duel. Whether the shooting occurred or not, Brown quit the army and, drifting to Alberta, built a log cabin on an embankment overlooking Lower Waterton Lake. He was a buffalo hunter (riding with the Métis), a peace officer (ending saloon brawls and jailing a counterfeiting gang), a gold prospector, a trading post proprietor, a militia scout, and an environmental crusader opposed to oil exploration in the Rockies. One summer Brown rode with the famous Pony Express. Crossing the Dog Den hills in Dakota Territory, he was captured by Sitting Bull and a warrior band. He was taken to a Sioux camp and stripped naked in readiness for a bonfire roasting. He rolled down an embankment, hid in a lake, and walked fifty miles to a fort.

Brown survived for another forty-eight years before dying in his sleep in 1916. Newspapers throughout the province recorded his passing with sorrow and praise. He was, the mayor of Pincher Creek stated, "an esteemed mountain man whose friendship everyone treasured." In other words, Kootenai Brown and the inhabitants of southern communities moulded a status that most misfits, past and present, envied — mutual acceptance.

Our second winter on the homestead commenced with an October blizzard and, producing its own kind of chill, a letter from Jessie's father. He had shot a moose and he was bringing us meat. He intended to stay for a week, sleeping in his camper-truck. I turned cold reading the letter, abhorring the prospect of my privacy being held hostage by a boozer given to rapid mood swings trickier to deal with than Judith Tyson's. "She broke my heart," he'd lament, tears glistening, remembering a girl who had jilted him in his youth. Seconds later, he'd be arguing with somebody and spoiling for a fight. In childhood, Jessie constructed the escape hatch she still ducked into whenever he became belligerent. "You can disagree with my father, but if he insists he's right, don't dig in your heels and insist he isn't," she warned me ages ago. "Even if he's saying something really exasperating, take a vow of silence and don't open your mouth."

9

Joe was in his sixties, a short, dense-chested person, arms and legs thickened by firm muscle. He conducted himself as though he had to prove he was the equal of men forty years his junior, which every now and then entailed punching a younger guy who hadn't been informed a vow of silence might spare him a slugging. Son-in-law or not, and despite sticking my tongue in a freezer when he was argumentative, I never doubted Jessie's dad would belt me if I angered him sufficiently. Occasionally, sensing that my silence was making him madder, I'd offer, "You have a point, Joe," or, in hope of introducing a new topic, I'd ask, "Have you shot anything interesting lately?" However, examining the motivation for my antipathy, I comprehended it was neither the threat of hard-knuckled aggression nor the mood jumping that troubled me the most. It was the impression that when Joe gazed in my direction, he saw, in his myopic assessment, a person failing to measure up. I was pale and scrawny and manually untalented; I didn't hunt, I didn't fish, I didn't brawl, I consumed only a single alcoholic drink a day and that

back
roads
Ted
Ferguson

drink was the nectar of the sissified male, a glass of white wine. The first time I met Joe he was standing on a bear-skin rug, the remnants of the six-hundred-pound grizzly that attacked him, and telling me what he thought of the lawyer handling his wife's portion of their divorce case. "That's no job for a man. He doesn't sweat; he doesn't dirty his hands. He sits at a blasted desk wearing shirts and ties and fancy suits, pretending he's a big shot. A phony bugger like that can't satisfy a woman. Balls are wasted on him. I'm going to cut them off and use them for door knockers." As I sat at a desk, sweat-free and clean handed, wearing shirts and ties and fancy suits, I instantly grasped that he wasn't just slagging my friend, he was serving notice that we weren't going to be buddies; I wouldn't be calling him Dad and he wouldn't be calling me Son.

Joe didn't respect me or my journalistic endeavours, and although the opinions of a narrow-minded person shouldn't have hurt my feelings, they did. I regretted Joe's dismissal because, the concealed truth was, I admired him. Jazz trumpeter Miles Davis was, by all accounts, a massive pain in the neck, yet listening to *Kind of Blue*, I quietly applauded the work of a master performer. Similarly, Joe was a master performer of outdoor pursuits. A one-shot hunter, a fisherman who seldom returned home without a solid catch, a fabulous cook whose recipes frequently featured elk and rabbit and porcupine. Skidding logs from the woods, he built a pleasant house a stone's throw from the Flathead River. To supplement his income, he was erecting a pair of log buildings to accommodate big-game hunters and to contain a tiny, rough-hewn café. He never got lost in the bush, but if he did, he knew which berries and plants were edible, which stars to navigate by, and how to create fishing lines, snares, and lean-tos.

Joe once owned a prosperous plumbing business. He resided in a grand split-level on a leafy Vancouver plateau and hob-knobbed with millionaires at a private skeet shooting club, parking his Indian motorcycle amid Cadillacs and Lincolns. Summer and fall, he'd whisk his wife to the Flathead on the bike, over four hundred miles of dust and wind and bouts of soaking rain. The wilderness made him happy; the city didn't. Maybe it was a subconscious goal, and maybe it wasn't, but either way, he played the horses and fat-stakes poker and, gambling his business into disarray, he moved to the mountains alone. Not that he was truly alone. His house was off a logging road that snaked between Polebridge, Montana, and Fernie on the Canadian side; friends were constantly dropping by, often in small groups, to pry open beer cans and converse in Bush Speak, a foreign language to anyone unfamiliar with woodsmanship and activities like repairing Ski-Doos and sump pumps. Joe was a mountain legend, a character known for his generosity, bawdy humour, and colourful hunting tales. Everyone enjoyed his company; no one was, like me, forcing themselves to tolerate him for their wife's sake.

I heard dogs barking.

I laid the book I was reading aside, prodded myself up from the chair, and went to the porch window. Joe's camper was in the yard. Rocky and Drake, black Labrador retrievers, were racing into the snow-struck bush, targeting an unseen foe. Joe climbed out of the cab, clutching a shopping bag. My wife and son were upstairs. I yelled that Joe had arrived and, plastering a fake grin on my face, I opened the door to welcome him. He entered the house shaking his head. "That's some road you built. I thought for sure a tree was going to break my side mirrors. Where's Jessie?"

"Right here," Jessie said, looming into the kitchen doorway. "Take off your boots. I don't want you tracking snow inside."

"It's water — it'll dry."

"It'll dry on the porch, not my floor."

Joe removed his boots and sheepskin-lined jacket. His chocolate brown shirt, dotted with cream-coloured triangles, and green polyester pants reflected the Flathead concept of dressing to the nines. His brown hair was barbered in the identical style it had been barbered since the Depression — severely short, scrupulously parted — and his nearly-shaven-to-the-bone face smelled of

back roads
Ted
Ferguson

an enthusiasm for Aqua Velva. The look and scent of the callous-handed class.

"This is real good," he said, plunking the bag on the table beneath the kitchen window. "Scenery for your meals."

"Yeah, it is nice," I said. "The snow storms are beautiful. Especially when you don't have to go out in them."

"I'm surprised you drove to the house," Jessie said. "I assumed you'd see the snow on the road and park by our truck. If it snows again, you might be stranded down here."

"No way. At your gate, I slapped chains on." There were twin bottles of Captain Morgan in the bag and a small gift, a Mason jar filled with relish he'd pickled. Joe twisted the cap off a rum bottle. "The meat's in the camper," he instructed. "Will one of you fetch it? I'm too tired."

The Labs were on the landing, shivering cold. I rubbed Drake's head and he sprang up, swishing his tail and pawing my clothing. I avoided Rocky. He was growling and baring his teeth — his infamous greeting for anyone who wasn't Joe. I fetched the moose meat and, retracing my steps, ushered the dogs into the house. Joe shouted for them to lie down and, marvellously trained, they sank to the porch floor.

"Twenty meals," Joe estimated, lounging at the table, drinking his mid-day booze mountain-style — straight, no mixer. "I had a bigger hunk in store for you, but you know those guys in the Flathead. Pete Wilson practically begged me for a piece, and the Wolf Girl wanted some, and Carl Swenson traded me a trout."

"This is plenty for us," Jessie said, extracting the canner from a lower cupboard. "Moose meat's very rich."

"Who's the Wolf Girl?" I asked.

"Government biologist. She's studying the wolf population. What's left of it to study."

His tone was impatient, edging on indifferent.

Questions from me bothered him. They forced Joe to acknowledge we were in the same room. They involved transferring his attention from a person who mattered to him, his daughter, and focusing on a person who didn't, his defective son-in-law. He spoke to Alex more than he did to me, but Alex was still on the periphery, excluded from the inner circle. Which was perfectly logical. Joe hardly knew the child. Born in Montreal, Alex was raised there and in Mexico and Vancouver. Joe visited us once in Quebec and a few times in Vancouver, and we spent a week together in the Flathead — an inadequate number of hours to secure the connection between grandfather and grandson. Joe admitted to Jessie that he was disappointed that our boy was a "stranger," and he pledged to take him to the Rockies when he was older and teach him hunting and fishing. For his part, Alex didn't feel he was missing out on a vital relationship. He had his parents, he had a grandmother in Vancouver, and he had friends at school. Joe was basically this old guy who disrupted his routine every couple of years, babbling and boring him. Far worse, his grandfather was, somewhere around his fifth drink, prone to grab him for a wet-eyed embrace he'd rather do without.

Knowing this, I appreciated why Alex took his time coming down from his bedroom to greet his grandfather.

"Here he is," Joe beamed. "The king of the castle. What were you doing up there, picking your nose and stuffing it in the pillow?"

"Listening to the radio."

"No homework?"

"I did it yesterday."

"Thataboy. I bet you're the head of your class."

"Not really."

"Your mom was bright in school. And Arlene. The brightest and the best looking. Everybody said so. Isn't that right, Jessie? Everybody said Joe's girls were the brightest and the best looking."

Alex plopped on a chair and waited for the limited range of comments adult visitors invariably pitched at him. You're taller than you used to be. I trust you help your mother a lot. Women will be swooning over you someday. You must be lonely with no brothers and sisters. Have fun now because when you're grown up and married you won't be having any.

I glanced at Jessie. She was squeezing meat into preserving jars and looking as though her father had already been with us half a century. Scanning the week ahead, all I saw was agony, perhaps larger amounts than I previously predicted. What I neglected to perceive was the chance that there was an element to Joe I knew nothing about, a characteristic capable of numbing the pain and reducing the distance between my father-in-law and myself.

"What does the clock say? Is it six?"

"Ten past."

"I'll get up and start the stove. Dad will be coming in soon. I don't want him harping on and on that people sleeping after six-thirty are lazy bums. Six-thirty is when he gets up, so it's when he thinks everyone should."

"I don't understand why you do this to yourself."

"Do what?"

"See your father at all."

"You were adopted and you never felt close to your adoptive parents. Blood ties are different. Remember our neighbours in North Van — the Watson's? The whole family gathers at Christmas and the two uncles inevitably wind up in a shouting match. The last time they almost came to blows over a business partnership that soured thirty years ago. This year the uncles will be celebrating Christmas together again, and next year, and every year afterwards. Because they're family. Because blood ties are special. Because they'll be attached to each other in perpetuity."

At 6:35 Joe strode into the kitchen gripping a Coors.

Jessie turned from the stove, spotted the beer and said with sharp disapproval, "For God's sake, father ..."

"For God's sake what?"

"Drinking before breakfast."

"No big deal, it's only beer." He took a sip and nodded towards the bathroom door. "The tub in there — you bathe in it?"

"Yes, dad, we're clean."

"We heat the water on the stove," I said.

"You scoop it out when you're done?"

"No, dad. We pull the plug and the water drains under the house."

"Crazy. You've got the pipes. Next summer I'll fix it so you can use it properly. The toilet, too. An outhouse in winter is like Jimmy Doolittle's raid over Tokyo. Drop the bombs and run. We'll rent a backhoe and put in a septic tank."

"How about the hole I dug?" I said, praying I had finally found a purpose for the aborted well. "Can it be a septic tank?"

Joe shook his head.

"Won't do." He sipped his beer and, addressing Jessie, said, "Lucky I brought the Winchester. There's a set of coyote tracks in your yard. Heading to the lake. A rancher by Kalispell pays bounty for dead coyotes. He won't know where I shot it, here or Montana."

"From what I hear, your buddies don't like shooting them, they prefer running over them with snowmobiles."

"Those kind of guys are no buddies of mine. The disgusting bastards terrify the poor animals chasing them till their lungs can't stand it and they fall to the ground. That isn't sportsmanship, that's cruelty. Anyway, those are them and this is me. No snowmobile, a rifle and a bedsheet."

"A bedsheet?" Jessie puzzled.

"Coyotes are slippery suckers. To kill them, you fool them."

After breakfast, I went upstairs to finish an article I was writing. My office overlooked the field and a portion of the frozen lake. Once in a while, I stopped typing and stared at the sunless landscape below the slope. Twice I sighted Joe. The first time, he made a slow, alert appearance from a shoreline thicket; he adjusted the white sheet draped over his head and shoulders, surveyed the area and stepped into the brush again. The second time, I was scrutinizing the trees and wondering where he was when he suddenly rose from the snow-covered ground, pointed the weapon, and then, lowering the barrel, dashed out of view.

Around twelve-thirty, Jessie called me to come down for lunch. Drake was stretching pleasurably in front of the hot stove; Rocky commanded a corner, sitting on his haunches, tense and suspicious. I was eating soup when Joe stomped onto the porch. The dogs barked and scurried to meet him.

"You miss me, boys? You miss Joe? I'm back now. Daddy's home."

Joe shed his boots and jacket and left them, along with the rifle and sheet, on the porch. He brought the dogs into the kitchen and ordered them to settle down. Drake chose the stove front; Rocky a different corner.

"I didn't get the coyote," Joe said. "He set eyes on me and ran like the wind. He's halfway to China. I nearly had him but I couldn't get a clear shot."

"I'll do a lunch for you," Jessie said. "Is chicken noodle soup and a ham sandwich alright?"

"Sure. Anything." He poured rum into a glass and asked her if there was a lumber yard in Sunnyside.

"No," I said. "In Preston."

"Down by the lake," he said, facing me, "I was thinking of the hole beside your house. Jessie will be planting in a garden next year. Sacks of potatoes and carrots. You'll be needing a cool place to store them so, why don't we turn the hole into a root cellar?"

In the country, waste is as rare as a beloved Liberal. Food scraps become pig food; egg shells, a garden nutrient; fatally stricken vehicles, spare parts supply depots; bales of straw, animal bedding. Converting the well pit into a vegetable storage unit suited the rural perception that nothing is useless except the idiot who throws it out.

With the cribbing already done, the conversion would begin with a fir floor and plywood shelving at the ten-foot level and proceed to fashioning a permanent ladder with two-by-fours. The above-ground walls, slanting, shingled roof and insulated, plywood door would follow. The root cellar and outhouse were of a similar design, resembling tool sheds, and while nobody but city-spoiled weaklings heated their outhouse, a kerosene lamp had to be kept in the root cellar on sub-zero nights. Constructing a root cellar was a fresh experience for my father-in-law, yet, gazing at the hole and the space above it, he quickly deduced the type and amount of lumber required and the manner in which it would all fit together. Gazing at the hole and the space above it, all I saw was a hole with space above it.

On our first day at the site, Joe was subdued and, eschewing alcohol, drank Cokes and tea. Hungover, I suspected. Either that or resorting to near-muteness to mask his revulsion over finding himself at close quarters with the lump of ineptitude his daughter married. When he did initiate conversation, primarily to render instructions, he was gently attentive, a personable teacher explaining complicated details to an equally personable student. He measured and sawed and hammered, completing the floor and starting the walls; I sawed and hammered, lowered flooring to him, and held the wall boards in place to be nailed. That evening, Joe reclaimed his usual, perplexing personality, stuffing Jessie's ears with sentences while cuddling Captain Morgan.

During the second day, witnessing a repeat of Joe's surprising transformation, I came to the gladdening revelation that he was neither hungover nor enacting an attentive-teacher role to hide revulsion. He was, plain and simple, a different person when he worked. Someone who, if not exactly a fun guy to be around, was level-tempered and considerate. At times, I wished my son wasn't at school so he could hang about the root cellar site, observing the other Joe, the grandfather, so that he could, as I did, feel less alienated by him. I suggested to Jessie that her dad and other people doing manual labour must be proud of their bodies and what they did for them. That, she said, was absolute nonsense. What their bodies did for them was manufacture sore backs, scars, and rough hands that irritated the women they touched. In her father's case, the pride came from doing it right, whether he was building a root cellar, hunting bighorn, or fixing somebody's plumbing.

Shoddiness was, in her opinion, repugnant to members of her dad's generation but deemed quite acceptable by a multiplying number of new-breed blue-collar tradespeople. Whatever motivated him, I found the other Joe to be so congenial that upon finishing the root cellar I invented chores for him — minor house repairs, a propane lamp installation, and building a set of front door steps, an unnecessary project considering the rear entrance was our customary route.

The night before he returned to the mountains, Joe said that if we didn't mind he was leaving "the boys" with us awhile. How long was awhile? Jessie queried. Well, he was keen on leaving Drake for good; the blasted dog was gun-shy and darted behind the couch when he grabbed a weapon off the rack. A Lab that was too chicken to hunt was a disgrace to his species. Was Rocky gun-shy too? No, sir, he was a fantastic hunter, but this broad he met was refusing to shack up with him due to Rocky terrifying her. Awhile in Rocky's case was for the duration of the affair.

"Okay," Jessie said. "If Ted agrees, we'll take them."

I agreed. When I was away, she'd be safer with dogs in the house. Particularly Rocky. Who'd willingly tangle with him? Certainly not me. I wasn't terrified but I was mighty leery. Rocky was a biter; he had recently wounded the fingers of a stranger who, disregarding Joe's warning, reached over to pet him. ("You won't hurt me, will you fella? You know I'm a pal.")

"Rocky's insane," I said to Jessie as we prepared for bed. "Have you seen his eyes? Charles Manson has a kinder look."

"He'll be fine," Jessie said. "My father's friends tormented him. Remember that guy in the Flathead dangling a hot dog from a branch and laughing when Rocky went hysterical trying to get it? We won't be dangling hot dogs here. The atmosphere will be calmer, and so will Rocky."

Late in January, a post office clerk pushed a large, manila envelope into the box just as I was about to clear out the mail. I smiled in thankful recognition; the envelope contained a balm for drooping mid-winter spirits, a glorious, ninety-page seed catalogue. I had been receiving the annual garden planner in Vancouver, but on the homestead, with water in restricted supply, its appearance was joyless, insignificant. Now, our circumstances had improved. Now, we had a well and on May 24th, the traditional date, we'd be planting an extensive garden close to it.

10

By the time I reached home, an ugly wind had risen, piling blowing snow into drifts, and the already inhumane temperature was intractably declining. Jessie was baking carrot muffins. She boiled water in the kettle, read a letter from her sister in Vancouver, and, over Earl Grey and muffins, we perused the catalogue. The illustrations were evocative — reds and purples, yellows and greens, blues and whites — and so were the descriptions. "A swath of enchanting blue colour." "The incomparable brilliance of scarlet red." "Gardens bask in the magic and majesty of these towering sunflowers."

Some seed catalogues, and there were dozens of them in North America, specialized in exotic flowers or numerous varieties of a particular vegetable. We spurned them; the run-of-the-mill fare, the plants we'd known since childhood, were fine enough for us. Still, the seed catalogue we received each winter wasn't above leaping into the arms of industry fads. Leafing through it, we noted that spaghetti squash and Chinese vegetables, trendy items in the past, were replaced by produce promising unusual colors — white eggplants, green radishes, lemon tomatoes, lavender pink pansies. None of the presentations warmed our stodgy hearts and, with a solitary alteration, Bibb lettuce instead of iceberg, we filled out the order form.

When the seeds arrived Jessie intended to transfer many of

them to milk cartons she had saved and, trimming a side off, converted into flats. In our house on the coast, she arranged the cartons on furniture and below windows, any spot trapping the sunlight the rain-soggy city dispensed in tight-fisted proportions. For a brief period, a half dozen flats perched on my desk beside my 1929 Underwood. This was distracting. I continually stared at the soil, wishing to witness that captivating moment when a plant pokes through, timidly, as if it is debating the pros and cons of leaving a nurturing environment.

The best gardener in the Dunes, the Polish Widow, also favoured the milk carton method. She scattered them throughout her dusty general store and the kitchen-bedroom combination beyond the ancient blanket-curtain. She was seventy years old, white-haired and lank, and strikingly eccentric. She donned deerskin leggings and a Canadian Army great coat in winter; broadbrimmed straw hats, ankle-length dresses, and Japanese slippers in summer. Her store, a small, weather-whipped frame building, was at the rim of the old highway; the exterior walls were blank, no evidence whatsoever of their mercantile status. Quite often, deciding the few customers the store drew were an unbearable nuisance, she bolted the door, sat at the counter knitting and ignored any knocking. Canned food, laundry soap (including a pre-war box of Rinso), and various nonperishable goods stood on crude wooden shelves. Bereft of electricity, she stashed Pepsi and ginger ale in cold-cellar water buckets. A mother requesting a Pepsi for her son was advised soda pop was foul for children and she wouldn't sell it to her; a man saying she looked marvellous for a woman her age was ordered off the premises because, she shrieked, she despised flatterers.

At the rear of the building, the Polish Widow grew a magnificent garden. Her vegetables were fat and healthy, her flowers tall and radiant. Contrary to the policy advocated by district gardeners, the Polish Widow planted the vegetables and flowers in the same rows. Clusters of snapdragons soared amidst carrots; petunias and pansies thrived in the potato patch. "Put marigolds with cabbages," she stressed. "Marigolds stop bugs in roots. Don't mix onions and garlic. They're like Deutschers and Frenchies — hate each other."

She treated her plants as though affection was a crucial nutrient. Employing an undisclosed system for differentiating between them, she termed some plants "he" and others "she." Inspecting a strawberry patch, she pointed at spreading tentacles and exclaimed, "Look, look, she's having babies!" Her advice to Jessie was to kneel in a row each day and passionately implore, "Grow big and strong for me. I am friend."

The Polish Widow's garden was impressively large, roughly two hundred square feet, but the wisest teacher I ever had, personal experience, enlightened me that a garden needn't be big to enchant the eye. Early in our life together, Jessie and I inhabited the upper floor of a nineteenth-century coach house on a midtown Montreal boulevard. Jessie grew carrots, lettuce, and herbs in a slender strip between the stone building and the popular thoroughfare. She bordered the plot with poppies, nasturtiums, and sunflowers. The red poppies and orange nasturtiums were pleasing, but the sunflowers out-shone them. Rising above the wrought-iron fence, their charming yellow heads could be seen half a block away. I was working at the CBC, a relatively easy job writing press releases and arranging celebrity interviews. My office was two blocks east of the coach house, and most days I'd walk home for lunch. Ambling up the boulevard under a hot noon sun, I delighted in spying the sunflowers, a singular splash of natural beauty amid clogged traffic and cheerless modern edifices.

We would be planting sunflower seeds next May, a long row beneath the back railings of the poplar fence I was scheduled to build. The Polish Widow's unorthodox approach, freely mixing vegetables and flowers, seemed madly incongruous, like inserting Gauguin nudes in a Constable landscape. Gladiolas, forget-me-nots, and their bright-crowned companions would be consigned to a special setting, a rock and shrub-studded enclosure on the south side of the house. Would the crops we planted near the well be as

back roads
Ted
Ferguson

successful as the Polish Widow's? I doubted it. The Polish Widow had her secrets, ancestral methods for fostering individual species, and although she did pass on some tips, she immediately appeared regretful, as though her tongue had spoken out of line and was being punished by her brain. Horticulture was, to her, a ritualistic practice akin to sorcery and, again similar to sorcery, to reveal its secrets might destroy her access to its powers. She hinted there was more to it than that — a mystical belief concerning the gods of nature and a familial pact — but we didn't press her. Nor did we attempt to squeeze more tips out of her, for we wouldn't be trying to duplicate the Polish Widow's proficiency. Our ambition was to pack the root cellar and, no less vital, to once more experience the uncommon pleasure American philosopher Amos Bronson Alcott was ruminating upon when he wrote, "Who loves a garden still his Eden keeps."

A high wind was howling across the flatlands, biting exposed flesh as though it hadn't eaten for months. An ideal day for Vernon Stubbs to laze indoors, drinking Ovaltine and watching *The Price Is Right*, activities his wife was engaging in when we reluctantly parted company with Frank's truck heater, negotiated an icy walk, and rapped on her front door.

11

"I figured you'd be coming another time," Adele Stubbs said as we stripped off our boots and jackets in the vestibule. "Darn cold out there."

"Doesn't faze me," Frank said. "After fifty-eight years I'm accustomed to it."

"It fazes me. Thirty-five below with the wind chill."

"We considered postponing," Jessie said. "We don't have a telephone. Frank showed up at our house so we thought, what the heck, we may as well go."

"My hubby's in the barn. Chores don't halt for bad weather."

Adele escorted us into the living room, her roly-poly body dipping from left to right and back again as if the balance mechanism was screwed up. She lowered the sound on the game show telecast but, fascination unabated, her gaze constantly skipped between her visitors and the murmuring screen. Adele and her husband had gone to school with Frank; the couple married in their teens, accumulated cash, and bought a farm south of Preston, off the Edmonton highway. Three years ago, Frank ran into Vernon on Palliser Street; they chatted for five minutes, sufficient time for Frank to feel justified in referring to him thereafter as "my friend Vernon."

"So you're starting a goat farm," Adele said.

"Maybe," I said. "Our minds aren't made up yet."

"I said to Frank on the blower we aren't selling any goats. The more goats, the more milk. The more milk, the more income."

"How many nannies do you own?" Jessie asked.

"Eighty-four. Listen, whatever you do, don't let Vernon catch you calling them nannies. He'll see red. Female goats are does. And males are bucks, so don't say billies."

"Eighty-four's sizable," Frank said.

"It's sizable, alright, but the bottom line is we don't make much of a living at it. We get by, and we're glad of that, but there's no money for extras. We haven't had a holiday for ages. A goat farm's a 365-day-a-year operation."

Myths and misconceptions are endemic to the farming profession, even more so, according to Adele, in attitudes and beliefs regarding goats. Goats don't eat tin cans. They chew the labels; the labels are paper, and paper's from trees, and goats snack on tree bark. Goats don't smell; bucks in a breeding mood do, but, like Frank and frigid weather, your nose becomes accustomed to it. Goats are vegetarians and won't gobble your pet gerbil. Goats can be trained to pull sleds and, if we were mounting a circus act, climb ladders and ring bells. Goats are mild mannered and won't bunt people unless people provoke them. "It's Hollywood cartoons that tagged goats with a nasty reputation. Cartoons and comic books. Somebody bends over and a goat bunts them. Who was it, Bugs Bunny? I don't recollect who, but I do recollect this cartoon when I was a girl where a goat breaks into a house and gobbles the contents. The curtains, the lamps, the pots and pans, the kitchen sink. Ridiculous. Just plain ridiculous."

"Nobody credits how smart goats are," Frank said, reaching for a favourite barnyard anecdote. "The opposite of chickens. I saw a chicken standing in pouring rain gawking at the sky. It hadn't the common sense to shut its mouth. It drowned itself. Filled its lungs with water and drowned itself dead."

"A goat won't do that," Adele said.

"What does goat's milk taste like?" Jessie asked. "Is it sweet?"

"No, not sweet. You can't tell the difference from cow's milk. And better for you. Pasturizing cow's milk they remove vitamins." *The Price Is Right* ended its daily reign. Adele switched the set off. "Milking's due. Try the milk for yourself."

We pulled our winter gear on and exited through the kitchen. The pathways were shovelled; salt was lavished upon ice patches. Identical-twin buildings — dull, grey cinder blocks — rose adjacent to a hip-roof barn, the milking parlour, and the pens. Adele left us, making her way, listing and breathing heavily, to the goats' residence. We proceeded to the parlour.

Vernon Stubbs was plugging a milking machine into a wall socket. He pivoted and nodded and said, "I saw your truck and said to myself, 'Those folks are immune to the cold. Doctors in Preston must be inoculating against it.'"

"Wouldn't that be swell," Frank said. "The miracle drug of the century. So how's it going, Vernon?"

"Fair to middling."

"These are the people I told you about on the phone."

"Pleased to meet you."

"It's a nice farm you have here," I said, for the sake of conversation.

"We think so. If you've got questions, fire away. I don't mind talking while I work."

Vernon was twice his wife's height and narrow-framed. His actions were casual and fluid, befitting someone performing repetitive tasks, yet, somewhat contrarily, he weighed his sentences as though rendering a misleading statement constituted a monstrous insult. He wasn't particularly friendly, nor unfriendly, towards Frank; he seemed to be a man who had committed himself to a rendezvous he wasn't thrilled by and, Prairie polite, he was seeing it through to the end.

"How much milk does a goat give every day?" Jessie asked.

"Quarts or litres?"

"Quarts."

"My top milkers, three, three and a half. Sometimes they slacken off but, by and large, goats are dependable. They're social, you understand. Goats will follow you to Mongolia and back. And they're affectionate, akin to cats. Your goat's depressed, it's feeling short-changed in the affection department. I'll tell you the remedy for that: hum a tune, rub its ears, and hug it."

"Is there one tune that works best?" Frank asked.

"*My Blue Heaven.*"

"I wonder if that would go over in the city," Jessie said humorously. "Humming, ear-rubbing therapists."

"I'm the wrong person to ask," Vernon said seriously. "City customs are beyond me."

I had a question. "With a herd this size, how long are the milkings?"

"Three hours, thereabouts. I don't clock myself. There's no foreman on this farm, nobody whipping me to speed up. I'm not slaving in a factory."

Nobody had to whip the goats to speed up. Adele dispatched the animals from the pens in groups and they zealously beelined to the parlour, many actually running. Mounting the stanchion's concrete platform, they shoved their heads past metal bars to dine on oats. Vernon attached the machines and pumped milk.

All of the goats were white. Saanens, Vernon said. A Swiss species with udders rivalling the queen of cows, the Holstein, in productive output.

"Mastitis is the scourge of the goat population," Vernon said. "The vet was here yesterday examining four cases. We may be losing a goat. Wasn't your boy going in for being a veterinarian?"

"No," Frank replied stiffly. "Doctoring. The medical type. Physicians and surgeons."

"The time we met in Preston, Greg dropped out of university for a spell. Is he studying again?"

"No, not yet."

"My boy's on the rigs. Couldn't make farming pay. Bill Morton bought his spread. He owns half the territory north of Exner. Corporate farming's the wave of the future, they say. The problem is, the wave's washing us minnows out to sea. How are the Fergusons bearing up? Are you kind of thirsty?"

He scooped milk from a bucket into a tin cup. Adele's expert opinion notwithstanding, there was a difference between it and the bovine brand. Goat's milk tasted a little richer.

"Liquid gold," Vernon said.

"I could drink this every day," Jessie said.

"So could I," I said.

I thought of Alex. Was it a drink he'd prefer? No, it wasn't. He'd prefer Coca-Cola, which, allowed free will, he'd pour on his cereal and in his soup and over his pasta sauce. Could I picture him consuming goat's milk without bitching? Yes. The taste wasn't so rich he'd deem it "yucky." My wife and I unreservedly agreed; next summer, we'd add goats to our shopping list.

Having nowhere he really needed to be, Frank was a slow driver, taking different routes to his normal destinations, scanning the summer countryside for alterations wrought by man and nature: a painted barn, an electrified fence, rain-flattened crops, anything worth telling his wife. There was far less for him to observe in winter, but he retained his insouciant pace, striving against the odds to distinguish something new in a landscape where nearly everything was on hold, waiting for break-up.

The goat farm served him well. So did the roads we took on the way home. North of the Stubbs' place we rode into a whiteout and, beyond the blinding storm, lumps of black ice the salt trucks hadn't attacked yet. Near the Sunnyside turnoff, Frank picked up three teenage boys whose Pontiac struck ice and lashed into a ditch. The youths huddled in the box, heads bent, hands in jackets, wretched to their roots.

"You happen to notice the tires on the Pontiac?" Frank said. "Bare as a banker's heart."

"A banker's heart?" I puzzled.

"Nothing in it."

"The tires have nothing in them?"

"Not in them, on them. They're bald, and bald tires don't grip. It's irresponsible to drive winter roads with them. Susan does it all the time. Pays ten bucks for junkyard tires with hardly any tread.

They're forever blowing out on her. She'd be wiser getting retreads, judging by the number of baldies she winds up trashing."

Junkyard tires wasn't the topic Jessie wanted to explore. She was curious about Greg's medical school sojourn. As Frank usually ducked personal discussions, she had decided in the milking parlour to wait until the Christmas season when Frank, ordinarily a light drinker, cadged free shots around town and, stoned by mid-afternoon, was apt to lower his guard. Now, with Frank mentioning his son, she surrendered to an impulsive tug and said, "I didn't know Greg studied medicine."

"He didn't say anything to you? Well, I guess I shouldn't be bowled over. It's a taboo subject in our family."

"Why is it taboo?"

"He quit before his degree."

"Did he run out of money?"

"No, that wasn't it." A tractor-trailer delivering a load of hogs was threatening our tailgate. Frustrated by Frank's slow progress, the driver blasted his horn and then, request denied, he blasted it again as he swooshed past us. Frank glared at the vehicle and said, "Silly bugger. He'll slide into a ditch and the truck will catch fire, but we'll be laughing — we'll have a ton of fried bacon to lug home."

We came to a service station. The teenagers scrambled off the box and, not even glancing at us, walked to the kiosk.

"Those kids will be glad to be warm," I remarked.

"Ungrateful brats," Frank said. "Three of them and not a solitary thank-you. I ought to boot their sorry rumps back to the Pontiac and strand them."

"If my son grew up to be like that," Jessie said, "I'd be wondering how I failed him."

"Yeah, well, Judith sure does."

"Greg isn't rude," I said.

"No. It's his schooling that tortures her."

"His schooling?"

"Judith counting on him going into medicine and becoming

a man she'd be proud of. She never dreamt she'd be giving him handouts at his age."

For Frank, that was an expansive disclosure. The exchange we had at the lodge concerning Judith's dad and her marriage to Frank was a quirky occurrence, a temporary collapse in his defence system. He hadn't been remotely near that forthcoming since then, and I accepted that he never would be. So I was surprised when he tapped the instrument panel with a gloved finger, causing the sticky fuel gauge to rise, and then, looking and sounding dismayed, he examined Greg's life history as if he was reading autopsy notes.

Greg was an outgoing child. In a likable way, not obnoxiously pushy. A carbon-copy, really, of Michael's personality. He was Greg's brother. Michael was two years older, a handsome lad. He died in an accident, four days short of his twenty-seventh birthday. When they were youngsters, Greg fancied what Michael fancied. If Michael fancied a fishing rod, Greg fancied a fishing rod. If Michael cared for cowboy movies, Greg cared for cowboy movies. One wouldn't go anywhere without the other. Frank dubbed them the Pea Pods.

Townsfolk probably think it was Michael overshadowing him that turned Greg shy. Maybe yes, maybe no. What's definite is Greg changed around the age of ten. He stopped speaking to people outside the family. He'd nod his head and grin and mumble. He wasn't the kid he used to be. Sentences no longer flooded out of him. His math teacher brought the change up at parent-teacher night, but she wasn't alarmed. His marks were high, so why push the panic button.

Judith is cautious with her money. Always was, always will be. But she was so overjoyed that her son was admitted to medical school that she got him the car he craved, the snazzy Mustang. The fact is, Judith was deadset on Greg doctoring, but he wasn't. He went to medical school due to her wanting him to. Greg was nuts about horses. He hung around the riding academy and private stables. Grooming horses, whatever. He skipped

back
roads
Ted
Ferguson

classes and couldn't concentrate in the classes he did attend. The professors scolded him, so he dropped out — and crushed his mother's heart.

"Something's gone from Greg and it isn't coming back," Frank sighed. "He's got no career path. No burning ambition."

No career path.

No burning ambition.

I gathered I was supposed to empathize with Judith, but I identified too closely with her son. My career path was foggy, my ambition was smouldering. I had no idea what happened to Greg's desire to succeed, whether it was his brother's death or a late-developing sensitivity to the universe at large, but I certainly knew what happened to mine. It washed away in the Vancouver rain.

Four years before moving to Alberta, I flew to the West Coast from Mexico with a wife and a son and sixty dollars. I wasn't worried about finding work and rebuilding my bank account. Traditionally, journalism in Canada was a free-flowing stream. Quit your job at a newspaper in the morning, you crossed the street and joined a competitor that afternoon. If by some slender chance the rival paper wasn't hiring reporters, there was journalism's venue of last resort, the tedious, perpetually short-staffed copy desk. For eight hours, you'd sit at a big, horseshoe-shaped desk writing headlines, editing stories, and faking a conviction that the nation's independence was jeopardized unless theatre and centre were spelled with "re" instead of the Yankee-doodle "er." Former star reporters, cynicism corroding their souls, languished alongside demoted newsroom executives, journalism school graduates with no talent for writing, guys penning mammoth, unpublishable novels in the wee, small hours and the odd man out, the true believer incensed by incorrect grammar and meaningless quotes.

Bill picked us up at the airport. He was an old friend from Montreal, an ex-journalist now practising criminal law. Walking to the parking lot, he said one of his partners was on a lengthy holiday in Europe and in exchange for babysitting his cat we could stay at his food-stocked house rent-free. The house was in Kitsilano, a rustic bungalow on a street of willows and hedges. Herbert, a fat tabby, ate gigantic amounts of Meow Mix, snored half the night and co-existed peacefully with pantry mice. One morning I sauntered into the pantry and accidentally stepped on Herbert's tail. He didn't yelp, he didn't run. He didn't do either of those things because he was dead. As there wasn't a mark on him, and because he was lying beside his bowl, I attributed his death to Meow Mix gluttony.

Herbert's owner phoned us each weekend to inquire about household matters. Bill's advice was not to inform him that the

12

back roads
Ted Ferguson

cat had died. He adored Herbert; we'd be blamed and evicted. A few days later, Bill's partner called. "What's Herbert up to?" he asked. "I'm not sure," I answered. "He's in the back yard at the moment." I didn't explain that he was buried there.

Herbert's passing was a turning point, not just for him but for me as well. I made an oath to never again rely so much upon another person's generosity — and never, ever, to put myself in a position where I had to hide the truth to elude eviction. With a living, breathing Herbert, I had delayed the job quest, waiting for the culture shock to dissolve. After three years in a Mexican hill town, I was wandering the city in a disoriented state, overwhelmed by the sheer multitude of material goods. With Herbert's death, I forced myself to seek employment, disoriented or not, to quicken our departure from the lawyer's bungalow.

Vancouver was a two-newspaper community, both owned by the same company. The *Sun* and the *Province* were on the same floor of a modern, Granville Street building. I phoned the *Province* and learned the paper was trimming its editorial staff. At the *Sun*, the city editor turned out to be someone I worked with in Montreal.

"We're in the midst of a hiring freeze," Patrick said, "but rest easy, I'll get you on somewhere."

Somewhere was the desk. For five weeks, I was lodged between a surly, gutter-mouthed, ex-religion columnist and a brash young woman whose only previous experience with journalism was sleeping with the editor who hired her. I was an incomprehensible weirdo to my desk mates: I appreciated having the job. The *Sun* generated the funds to leave the dead cat and the bungalow and to lease our own rustic house on our own street of willows and hedges. When a reporter retired, Patrick plucked me off the desk. I covered luncheon speeches, suburban council meetings, and flying-saucer sightings. Two months later, the television columnist resigned, creating an opening for what was considered a plum position, a belief unrelated to the salary increase or its value as a platform for influencing public opinion. The television columnist got to stay home; a company car picked up his copy and delivered his pay cheque. Most of the people on the desk and four veteran reporters applied for the job. Assigning it to me, the managing editor confessed he was choosing the newest kid on the block, for if he selected one long-term employee over the others, the newsroom would be poisoned by bitterness.

The column took two to three hours to write. After the *Sun* car retrieved my nocturnal musings, I lingered in the kitchen, fully awake, chomping crackers and cheese, careful not to disturb my slumbering family.

Attempting to exhaust myself, I tried jogging along deserted suburban thoroughfares but, hating all that jiggling and jarring, I retired my sneakers. I delved into ponderous classics, stumbling and falling during the early chapters of *Remembrance of Things Past* and *The Red and the Black*. French language lessons on an album of second-hand seventy-eights made me restless, as did late-night repeats of *Gilligan's Island* and *I Dream of Jeannie*. All else failing, I turned to writing.

I wrote television and radio dramas and CBC comedy sketches. Magazines bought my articles. I contributed a toothless gossip column to a monthly magazine under a pseudonym, The Snooper. Work begets work, and I was soon helping TV yoga teacher Kareen Zebroff launch and operate an alternative health monthly. The money gushed in and the money gushed out; a sizable portion of it vanished into a disastrous enterprise, an arts and entertainment journal.

Sleep became an annoying intervention, disrupting my labour for four or five hours. Some people's internal mechanisms are designed for workaholism. Nerves of oak, bloodless and cool. I deceived myself into imagining I was one of them. In my second year of intense toil, itchy, red rashes appeared and disappeared on my neck and chest; an eyelid twitched for a couple of weeks, ceased for months, resumed twitching again. Thumping headaches were a nuisance. Aspirins fixed the problem, so I swallowed them at regular intervals, before the black clouds had a chance to assemble.

back roads
Ted Ferguson

Travelling in a taxi to interview a TV celebrity, I grew dizzy and broke into a clammy sweat. I reclined on the seat, and when the episode ended I assured myself that an influenza virus had romped through my system. Weeks afterwards, I began to experience periodic trembling spells and sometimes, at cocktail parties and business meetings, the back of my neck stiffened. Finally, I admitted to my wife and myself that stress was assailing my body, but, having a somewhat perverse attachment to my heavy workload, I protected it as if I was embracing an ailing child. Stress was an unavoidable condition in North American society, I said, and I had to learn to live with it.

On my wife's birthday, we went to a rooftop restaurant with another couple. In the lobby, approaching the elevator, I was suddenly, inescapably petrified of being so high off the ground. By the time we alighted at the twelfth floor, my legs were shaking. The maitre d' led us to a white-linen table by a window. What a great panorama, Jessie said. It's beautiful, Angela said. Height gives you a unique perspective on a city, Bruce said. I nodded and agreed with the three of them, even though I was encased behind thick walls, isolated and terrified. We ordered drinks and hors d'oeuvres. Angela said she preferred Victoria to Vancouver, and Bruce said he was quitting his newspaper job and settling in England. I said little, I ate little. I stared at the tablecloth, palms sweating, heart thumping. The window was an object of horror; a single glimpse and I was certain I'd panic and faint.

I picked at the main course. Jessie asked, sotto voce, if I was feeling okay. Yes, I lied. A bit tired, that's all. Bruce revealed he was a champion athlete in his college days. Angela disclosed she was legally separated from her wealthy husband. I got up and pointed myself towards the washroom. My legs weakened. Realizing I was about to fall onto a candle-lit table and a quartet of gleefully chattering diners, I abruptly sat down on the carpet. The quartet's babble dangled incomplete. I lifted an arm and waved to gain Jessie's attention, an unnecessary gesture for my sitting on the floor in the middle of a five-star restaurant was a fairly effective attention-getter. A waiter pulled me up. Jessie and Bruce gripped my arms and assisted me to the elevator. Eyes shut, I leaned against a panel and sweated each and every inch of the descent. Hailing a cab, I regained self-control, joking that the next time I ate at that restaurant I'd bring a stretcher.

"You have to go to a doctor," Jessie said as we prepared for bed.

"I don't need to. I know what's wrong. I'm working too hard."

"Then stop doing it."

"I will. I'll scale back."

"When?"

"Right away. Before the stress does something really serious."

Scaling back right away was an impossibility; I had commitments, deadlines. But I did reduce the load, gradually, fluidly, and with the work-drug wearing off, I examined my life in a brighter, sharper light. I saw what the addiction had cost me. We inhabited the same house — sleeping, eating, bathing — but I was a man in a glass cage, seeing and hearing, yet separate, disconnected. A victim of parental neglect, I grew to manhood swearing that if I married and had children I would be a flawless husband and dad, eclipsing Robert Young, surpassing Danny Thomas, making all of the tv fathers seem like studies in domestic inadequacy.

That pledge had died, starved and battered by ambition. I yearned to resurrect it; I yearned to be close to my family again. The easiest, most logical course was to revert to the way things were before I entered into the workaholism cage. Write the tv column and devote the remainder of my waking hours to Jessie and Alex. Easy and logical didn't appeal to me. I was inclined to cut and run. The ageless philosophy that you can't run away from your problems was a crock of crap, an assumption likely invented and marketed by a group of pre-Christianity merchants fed up with fleeing employees forcing them to spend money on retraining programs. Dashing to the nearest exit was, in my experience, a life-enhancing method, even if it involved sacrificing a meaty pay cheque.

back
roads
Ted
Ferguson

I resolved to get out of Vancouver. Jessie, an inveterate rambler who felt at home anywhere in the world, was all for it.

We considered a village near Kyoto. We could tap our savings to launch a business peddling plaster replicas of a Canadian the Japanese idolized as though she were a deity, Saint Anne of Green Gables. Cuba was a second option. We could teach English to government bureaucrats and tourist hotel staff. Neither of us was a Communist, but the *Internationale* had a crackjack melody so we wouldn't balk at singing it in May Day parades.

Susan's letter eliminated those half-cooked alternatives. Mailed days earlier in Alberta, it was, like all of Susan's missives to us, a bearer of nostalgia, for it instantly revived images of colonial buildings, cobblestone streets, and bougainvillea-blessed courtyards. Jessie and I had gone to San Miguel de Allende on a six-month sabbatical and, loving the town, we did what we could to survive financially after postponing our return to Canada. I wrote a trashy memoir for an American publisher, *My Lesbian Secrets,* under a female nom de plume and Jessie, a weaving student at the *Bellas Artes,* created wall hangings and scatter rugs a local shop sold as the work of a Mexican artisan. Susan had won a trip to Mexico in a radio station draw; Greg and she were in San Miguel for only a month, and as we had numerous friends among the long-term foreign populace, we thought of them as passing acquaintances, an agreeable couple we'd never see again once they flew home. We had dinner at their apartment and attended a fiesta and went to the hinterlands church where, combining Catholicism and pagan beliefs, parishioners deposited dead birds on the altar and knelt at the foot of a statue of Jesus adorned in a robe embroidered with intimidating eyes.

The letters Susan dispatched to Jessie every year or so were always regurgitating the groovy time we had together in Mexico.

This letter was different. This letter was about the Dunes.

"The summers here are out of sight. We pick wild berries and swim at the lake and sometimes we just lie on our backs in a field, looking at the big, blue sky. How are you guys doing? Are you rolling in dough? The municipal district's auctioning a quarter section in the Dunes. I charmed a clerk into telling me the highest bid so far is twenty-four hundred bucks. Really cheap, and Greg and I thought you might like to buy it as an investment. If so, send me a cheque before the first of next month and I'll score it for you."

We hesitated, and not because of an absence of trust.

If we bought the land, it wouldn't be an investment; it would be a place to live. We talked and talked, debating the delights and disadvantages: wild berries and swimming holes versus wicked winters and low-income jobs. When Jessie was reading a magazine article on Isak Dinesen, she saw a quote that helped terminate the debate: "If you want the gods to laugh, tell them your plans." The gods had laughed hearing us discuss Havana and Kyoto and, in a sympathetic gesture, they devised a sensible escape route. They nudged Susan into sending the letter.

The gods spoke and we listened.

We mailed the cheque to Susan.

back
roads
Ted
Ferguson

13

Not long after we settled in the bush, my futile expeditions criss-crossing the quarter section dreaming of discovering a natural spring expanded into routine hikes far past the barbed wire boundaries of our property. I wandered for miles, on sleepy roads and in calm woods. In *Paradise Lost*, Milton wrote, "For solitude sometimes is best society, And short retirement urges sweet return." My sweet return transpired almost every rainless day I was home between spring and winter. Deprived of that pleasure after the snows deepened, I finally lit upon a system for slamming winter to the mat: I took up cross-country skiing. On foot or on skis, the habitual excursions were a private affair, an intimate space that no one, not even my family, ventured inside. I was alone but I didn't feel lonely. People suffering spasms of abject restlessness when they were alone in the wilderness were people bored with themselves. Solitude was a privilege, not a punishment. Solitude cleansed the soul. Solitude invigorated, restored.

Those were late-blooming observations, germinating seeds planted in my youth and largely forgotten. Residing in jammed, blaring cities, just another spoke in the commercial wheel, I envied anyone with access to nature and the benefits of soli-tude. Hemingway and his Michigan cottage, Van Gogh at Arles, Thoreau and his famous pond. In my twenties, I played with the naively romantic idea of joining the Moses-bearded monks at Mount Athos. I wasn't religious and I couldn't fathom a word of Greek, but the photographs I'd seen in a travel book forged the impression that the mountainous peninsula offered a more enchanting atmosphere than the office I worked in. A splendid, tenth-century monastery nestled below a craggy cliff. A bespec-tacled monk scrutinized a scrolled manuscript in an ancient library. Olives ripened in a sunny grove; monks carted baskets of freshly harvested figs. Offshore, a weathering fishing boat navigated the blue Aegean. German author Erhart Kästner was quoted as saying, "Athos is a pool of stillness in the midst of our talkative, preoccupied, relentlessly busy world." Dumped by a girlfriend, I earnestly contemplated licking my wounds at the holy retreat. I envisaged myself uttering obligatory morning prayers, and then enjoying Mozart and Art Tatum LPs in my sea-view cell prior to a meditative hike and, if those morning prayers were answered, a liaison with a sultry village girl. A research mission to a neighbourhood library crushed the Athos illusion. All females, including female animals, were banned from the peninsula. Monastery dwellers locked themselves into chanting marathons where they repeated a single-sentence plea for divine forgiveness. Cliffside caves throughout the peninsula housed religious loonies — many, no doubt, casualties of excessive chanting — and at some of Athos' two dozen monasteries, the meals were skimpy and bland.

In Alberta, solitude came on my own terms.

Valuing the silence, I refrained from carrying a cassette player and earphones and, unlike seventeenth-century philosopher Thomas Hobbes, whose walking stick was equipped with an inkhorn, I didn't take pen and paper to scribble notes. As I never met anyone hiking the country roads, I assumed I had an even slimmer chance of meeting a fellow walker in the woods. (Who, besides myself, had faith in the admittedly shaky theory that bears and bobcats and vicious wild dogs ducked contact by scampering deeper into the bush upon detecting a human scent?) I was tramping a deer trail edged by spruce and fir, en route to the Polish Widow's store, when I spotted a white-haired man seated against a tree, holding a canteen to his mouth. Drawing near, I recognized the retired civil servant I glimpsed once in a while in the yard of the pink house on the highway. A recluse, Frank had said. A bachelor with an embittered disdain for the medical system incapable of curing his arthritis. Frank had gone to the pink house seeking water for a volcanic radiator. He knocked and knocked and when he finally opened the

back
roads
Ted
Ferguson

door, the recluse was icy and gruff. Three in the afternoon and he was wearing pyjamas.

"I'm sorry," I said. "I didn't mean to wake you."

"Wake me?'" he said. "Are you balmy? It's three in the afternoon."

He smelled awful, like he hadn't washed since they pensioned him off. When he went for the water, I was dying to say, "I can wait if you care to use the first bucket on yourself."

I greeted the recluse cordially. Some people had mercurial natures, cold one minute, boiling the next, and it was a mistake to prejudge a person's reaction based on someone else's version of a brief encounter.

"What a lovely day," I said. "Great for the crops. Rain in the morning and now all this sunshine."

"You know me?"

"You're the guy with the pink house."

"Don't go tearing into me about that," he said, drawing himself erect. "Pink was the colour when I bought it."

"I'm not tearing into you."

"I'm here for the peace and quiet," he said, looping the canteen strap around his neck. "I'm not fixing to make a friend."

Peace and quiet? Living by himself, he must receive an ample dosage of that — unless the handful of vehicles passing his house hourly sounded like the Indy 500 to him — unless the croaking frogs and buzzing mosquitoes in the bog behind the Pepto-Bismol bungalow were abnormally loud?

"Okay, I won't bother you," I said.

"I don't talk for the sake of talking," he said as I plunged ahead.

I chanced upon the chronically frosty recluse one more time. It was autumn, the air was clear and perky, and I was on the road around the point where the deer trail cut into the woods. He appeared at the cusp of the trees. Is that what he does? I wondered. Go to the same spot over and over? From now on, I'll avoid the deer trail and, with luck, avoid him. He watched me pass. He didn't nod, he didn't raise his hand; he watched as if I was a dust devil he was hesitant to be caught up in. Insults rolled through my head. Miserable bastard. Pathetic old fart. I stifled the impulse to berate him. He was prickly and rude but I had to respect him, however begrudgingly, for we were birds of a feather, and a rare species, both prizing a discipline modern civilization attached little worth to: walking in solitude.

14

Preston was whooping it up. An orderly, restrained whoop for the town fathers and the local merchants association, copying the formula established for Frontier Daze's inaugural session seventeen summers ago: forbid alcohol at public events, riding horses downtown, and "unbecoming conduct" by spectators during tire-rolling and married-couples sack races. Old West facades and cutesy signs decorated main street buildings: Harlan's Drugmart was the Snake Oil and Love Potions Apothecary; the Preston Hotel was the Thirsty Rattler Saloon; Kathryn's Ladies' Apparel was Calamity Jane's Fancy Duds. Inside the buildings, management and staff draped themselves in cowboy garb — some wore toy six-shooters and phony sheriff's badges — and the ubiquitous greeting was a cheery, "Howdy, partner." Employees were encouraged to have fun but the fun was strictly controlled. A young teller aiming a plastic pistol at customers and declaring, "Hands up!" was advised by the manager that a bank was an inappropriate setting for her infantile joke.

Frontier Daze itself was, to my mind, an inappropriate joke. Preston and the encircling prairie had never been cowboy country. The pioneering settlers were principally Scottish and Ukrainian farmers and I was sure not many of them strapped six-shooters over kilts and sheepskin coats. I was tempted to express that view to Wally Gossip, but I held my tongue, wary of having him spread the word that I was the worst kind of citizen, an enemy of community spirit.

"So how are you folks keeping?" Wally asked.

"Wonderful," Jessie said.

"This is my lunch hour," Wally said, as though he was legally contracted to explain his presence. "One to two."

"It's five past two," I said.

"I'm the acting assistant manager. I'm entitled to bend rules. Not a bad crowd, eh? For a weekday."

We were standing on the sidewalk outside Chuckwagon Chow (Wong's Café). Fifty or so revellers were milling about booths and tents on the closed-off street, consuming pancakes and lemonade, playing games, scooping up household knick-knacks, visiting the gypsy-costumed fortune-teller. Proving he was the best kind of citizen, Wally wore a white Stetson, a western shirt, and a felt vest bearing a US Marshal badge.

"Frontier Daze must be a shot in the arm for local stores," I said.

"Sandy McDonald at the drug store says his profits rose five percent. There's a bunch of tourists in town. I saw two cars with Saskatchewan plates. Far as I know, we've had only one bit of trouble. Freddy Mazankowski and Cliff McGregor brawling at the square dance. I say, you feel like fighting, go home and fight with your wife. Don't spoil other people's night out."

I had no idea who Freddy Mazankowski and Cliff McGregor were, but I understood that knowing the scrappers' names was important to Wally. Maintaining his reputation as the town's most knowledgeable information dispenser required details. With my aversion to being squeezed for recyclable gossip, I normally tried to dodge the flappy-lipped snoop, but today, obeying a self-serving impulse, I deliberately approached him. No one I already asked knew where we could obtain goats.

"We want to get some goats," I said. "You happen to know anybody selling them?"

"Goats? You going in for witchcraft?"

"Unfortunately, no," Jessie said. "Witchcraft's probably a rewarding hobby."

"Feedlot's the place."

"We dropped by there on our way to town," Jessie said. "They don't handle goats." "The fellow telling you that — did he look like a St. Bernard?"

"I don't think so," Jessie said. "He wasn't slobbering."

"Hairy, chunky, dark eyes?"

"Yes."

"Leo Bouchard. He hates women. Won't even talk to his mother.

He'd have said anything to be rid of you. Speak to Brad. He's the head honcho. You can spot him a mile away. Big guy, brushcut, jelly-belly. He tolerates women."

We revisited the feedlot.

The hairy, bulky-bodied misogynist was hosing a cattle truck. He paid no attention to us. I drove to the office, an aluminum trailer on cinder blocks, in front of a cluster of pens and ramps and a small corral. Cattle savoured pasture grass in the near distance and, well past them, buffalo collected. The buffalo had grazed in a field facing the highway until a motorist jumped out of his car to snap a picture. The flashbulb panicked the animals; they smashed the wooden fence and chased the vehicle.

A brushcut, jelly-bellied man was seated behind a glass-topped desk, slumping in a swivel chair, phone in hand. There were family pictures on the desk, *Playboy* centrefolds on the walls.

"First in calf-roping and first in steer-riding," Brad bragged into the mouthpiece. "Yeah, I'm a helluva happy camper. Gotta go. Business before pleasure." He hung up, tilted forward and said, "My boy did good at the Little Cowhands Rodeo."

"Congratulations," I said.

"Chip off the old block. I won those events at his age."

"We're looking for goats," I said. "We're thinking of breeding them and selling the kids to diary farmers."

"How many you after?"

"Two to begin with."

"Nannies?"

"Yes. If goats are as easy to live with as people say they are, we'll gradually increase the flock."

"You must've been born under a lucky star. Two nannies is what I've got."

We accompanied Brad to a pasture behind a barn. The goats were tethered on twenty-foot chains. The larger of the two, a brown Toggenburg, commenced bleating the second it laid slanted eyes on Brad. The white Saanen shook its head and yanked its chain gallows-tight.

"The ladies are eager," I said, wondering what they were eager about.

"They don't take to tethering," Brad said. "I had to do it. Goats glue themselves to people. It drove my men nuts, goats on their heels."

"How much are you asking?" I inquired.

"Sixty apiece."

"Oh. I was counting on a cheaper price."

"The fellow selling them to me said they were good milkers, which is why I set the price at sixty each. Tell you what I'll do. You seem like an okay couple, so why don't I make it ninety for the pair."

"I'll go along with that."

"Where's your farm?"

"The Dunes."

"I'm sending a man to pick up a mare in New Hamburg. I'll have him load the goats and tail you out."

"Terrific," I beamed. "Fresh milk. We don't have a fridge so we've been using the powdered stuff."

Jessie was less joyful.

"I'm not sure about this," she said in the Black Bobcat. "He lowered his price awfully fast and he's delivering them right away. I hope nothing's wrong with the goats."

"They looked all right to me."

"Just because they weren't rolling on the ground and yelling for a medic doesn't mean they aren't ill. Maybe the bigger one was bleating because her brain tumour's hurting."

"In a small town a reputation for dirty dealing can destroy a business. Brad wouldn't risk it. He wouldn't sell sick animals."

When the goats arrived at our homestead, they streaked to the trees at the edge of the yard and stood, taut and guarded, appraising us and their surroundings. As the horse trailer ascended the hill, I walked over to them. I petted the Toggenburg, hand-fed her and the Saanen poplar leaves. The dogs were barking. They heard the vehicles and wanted out of the house. Jessie went to release them. Copying the goats, I was anxious. Rocky still growled if

back
roads
*Ted
Ferguson*

anyone tried to touch him, but immersed in a calmer environment, he was, as my wife predicted, noticeably more relaxed, sprawling on floors and no longer sitting in corners. Nevertheless, he worried me. He had a history of attacking bears and coyotes, and I was afraid he'd rocket to the goats and rip into them. Instead of milk in the morning, we'd be nailing trophy heads over the porch door, like Jessie's father did.

Jessie freed the dogs. "Rocky, sit," she commanded. He ignored her. Both dogs raced down the stairs. The Saanen darted further into the bush. The Toggenburg held her ground, bending her head, ready to bunt. Drake didn't worry me. He was intelligent and, I figured, he'd realize we weren't alarmed by the goats arrival so why should he be. "Rocky, sit!" Jessie yelled from the porch landing. "Do you hear me? Sit!" Mercifully, Rocky pulled up short of the goats and dropped onto his haunches. Tail swishing, Drake stopped beside me and then, as the Toggenburg stepped closer, positioning herself for a bunt, he shied away.

Alex was fascinated by the goats. Discovering they'd trail him wherever he went, he'd dash onto the field, pivot, and dash back, the goats in excited pursuit. Through with sprinting, he conducted dietary experiments, feeding the Toggenburg a Coke bottle (sniffed and rejected), the Willie Nelson eight-track (sniffed and rejected), a smelly sock (sniffed and rejected), and a newspaper culinary column (sniffed, chewed, and swallowed).

"Can I ride them?" he asked his mother.

"No."

"Can we take them to Sunnyside to show my friends?"

"No."

"Can I tie streamers to their horns?"

"No."

"Can I name them?"

"Yes, that you can do. You can name them."

Twenty minutes later, he unveiled his selections. Maya for the Toggenburg (in honour of Mexico) and Bella for the Saanen (in honour of Bela Lugosi).

"Those weren't my favourites. Dad won't go for the others."

"What are they?" his mother asked.

"Satan's Sister and Evil Eyes."

"You were right," Jessie said. "We won't go for them."

The next morning, Alex and I milked the goats. Bella was first. Alex fed her oats while I knelt, a plastic pail under her bags. I had practised on Greg and Susan's cow and learned you didn't grab the teats and squeeze as energetically as possible, you gripped the top and pulled firmly downward. Bella was patient, consenting to my amateurish technique, but the amount of milk she contributed was forlornly slight, scarcely covering the pail bottom. Maya's bags were fatter. We repeated the procedure, Alex on oats, me on teats. The initial pull yielded a strong stream — and a twisting, bucking, bleating rebellion. When I let go, she stood still. Alex whispered reassuring words of affection plus a plea to liberate him from powdered milk. I stroked her ears and hummed *My Blue Heaven*. When I crouched, adjusted the bucket and grasped her teats, she staged a second uprising. We tried the routine again, with a similar outcome.

I retreated to the house.

"We'll milk her tonight," I said to Jessie. "She'll be fine once she becomes accustomed to the idea."

At dusk, the three of us converged on Maya. Jessie held her horns; Alex talked quietly to her, a soothing monologue concerning good and evil and how he understood that, in her heart of hearts, she yearned to be good and bless us with an ocean of milk; I pulled her teat. She wriggled and bucked and bitched.

"Maybe it's paining her," I sighed. "Maybe we did buy a medically unfit goat."

"Let me try," Jessie said.

She knelt on the ground and started milking. Maya was silent, almost motionless. Jessie laboured until the flow dried up. The amount in the bucket was unimpressive, perhaps enough to fill a pint jar. Jessie tried Bella next; her second contribution of the day was enough to fill a shot glass.

back roads
Ted Ferguson

"Maya wasn't hurting," Jessie said. "She just didn't like your hand. She craved a feminine touch. You know, females together — women bonding — that sort of thing."

Frank showed up three or four days afterwards.

"We milk the goats around dinner time," I said to him. "The Toggenburg gives us a pint. We've stopped doing the Saanen. If there's milk in her, she's hoarding it."

"Their bags are on the small side. I mean, compared to the nannies at my friend Vernon Stubbs' farm."

"We're taking them back to the feedlot. He must have known they were poor milkers. That's why he was eager to get rid of them."

"Did he write you a receipt?"

"Yes."

"Read the wording. All sales final. That's what it says, and Brad won't relent unless you're a customer for donkey's ages, which you aren't."

"So we're stuck with the goats."

"Not necessarily. There's a sure-fire answer to your predicament."

"What's that?"

"Shoot them."

"Shoot them? God, I can't do that."

"Well, they might be bigger milkers once they're bred. I recall somebody somewhere claiming that happens sometimes."

I was in the garden, hoeing weeds, when the Mustang descended the hill and swept into the yard. The dogs were lying outside the garden fence, the goats strolling the unplowed field, sampling wild plants here and there like professional wine-tasters. Drake bolted to his feet and barked vigorously. Rocky snarled. The goats tightened and gaped. Susan slipped off a bucket seat and, waving towards me and the staring dogs, sauntered to the house. She was, I found out later, delivering a loaf of bread: a new recipe she baked in her oven that, winning Greg's approval, she determined was a discovery worth sharing.

15

I kept hoeing. For decades after an unknown farmer last planted and harvested a crop on the field, weeds ruled the space we designated for the garden and, ousted by our family in the spring, they were fighting to regain power. The crabgrass fought harder than the other usurped rulers. It possessed a salamander-like ability to regenerate itself; we had to shovel deep, to the tips of the roots, and rip each piece out individually. We did that probably eight dozen times, and almost as often, we studied the rows, deemed the garden a crabgrass-free zone, and then, cruelly, belligerently, it reappeared. There were insects as well — tiny, black leaf-eaters — and bush rabbits that attacked the lettuce, but all and all, our first garden in Alberta was coming along nicely, an agreeable vision to present to Susan, which I gathered I would be doing before she went home. Looking at other people's gardens was a common practice in farm country. Invite someone over to admire your newest acquisition — a bedroom suite, a car, a stereo — and regardless of how bowled over they were, they inevitably wished to investigate how you were measuring up where it truly counted, in the garden. Green-thumbers were treated like members of a special corps, Mother Earth's hand-picked elite. The corps leaders — those capable of growing mammoth, medal-meriting vegetables — received what many people thought was a great honour, being mentioned in dispatches from Wally Gossip's active mouth. Black-thumbers — the gardeners with dinky carrots or miscarrying squashes — were scorned as if they insulted the soil and should be denied future access to seeds.

Our garden wasn't spectacular, nothing rating a Wally mention, but Susan was always impressed. She had witnessed the slow, aching-body change from solid, weed-packed dirt to promising sprouts and, on her last visit, to a state where the plants burst forth and assumed familiar shapes. Now they were double that size and awesomely healthy.

The hoeing done, I walked over to the well and, drawing the bucket to the surface, filled the garden pails. The pails needed to stay in the sun until the late-afternoon watering. ("Well water cold," the Polish Widow said. "Sun licks water and plants don't shiver. Plants love you for this.") The pails loaded, I checked to ensure the chicken-wire barrier we secured around the foot of the garden fence to thwart the rabbits was intact. I was tempted to expand the inspection tour to the hay pile at the rim of the field, but recalling Ruth Stout's warning against exposing concealed crops to sunlight, I dissuaded myself. Stout was a New Englander, the ninety-six-year-old creator of a mulching, no-digging system of gardening. I read an article in which she advised horticulturists to heap vegetable wastes and leaves together in the autumn and, come spring, to rake them aside and insert seeds by hand in the soft earth. Furthermore, some vegetables could be grown without being planted at all; simply blanket them between layers of decomposing hay. I was testing her method. I had shoved twelve seed potatoes inside a pile of rotting hay; a topping of coal dust and goat turds discouraged cleanliness-obsessed Maya and Bella from disturbing the pile.

Drake heaved himself up again, barking, wagging his tail.

Jessie and Susan were on their way down.

I returned to the garden and began transferring the slain weeds to the wheelbarrow.

"Wow," Susan said. "You guys are really super at this."

"Jessie's the gardener," I said. "I help with the brainless labour."

"I can't get Greg in our garden. He's busy carving. He's making a cowboy on a horse. What's that stuff surrounding your cabbages? Is it ashes?"

"Yes, ashes," Jessie said. "From the kitchen stove. The Polish Widow swears the bugs won't cross them. So far, she's right. I haven't seen any on the cabbages."

"Groovy."

The loaf of freshly baked bread wasn't all that Susan brought to our house. She was a conveyer of news. Yesterday, north of Preston, she spied a sign on a farmer's gate advertising a "moving to Manitoba" auction sale. The farmer's teenage son was by the barn, washing a tractor. She drove onto the property to ask if his parents were selling their living room furniture. Her mission that summer was to replace her ragged, wine-stained sofa. The boy retrieved an auction list.

"The furniture wasn't on it," she said, "but I saw something you guys need. A full-size propane refrigerator. They used it at a cottage that belonged to them."

"When's the sale?"

"Next week. But you don't have to go. The boy said his dad's hungry for cash. Offer him thirty bucks and he'll leap at it."

"We'll drive over tonight."

The two women walked to the far end of the field where, from a different angle — the top of the incline — the lake and hills lengthened, becoming more languorous, more compelling. I went to the house and, mounting the stairs, settled at the Underwood. An hour or so later, I heard the Mustang shoot up the hill and then Jessie came inside.

I descended the stairs.

"You were gone a long time," I said.

"We were talking."

"Susan never says anything serious."

"Today she did. She was in a funny mood. Frank was at her place this morning and Greg wouldn't look at him. It's the anniversary of his brother's death. Frank usually doesn't show his face on this day, but he probably didn't realize what the date was. You don't have a regular job, you're fuzzy on dates."

"I guess we'll never know why Michael's death created the friction between Greg and his father. Frank certainly won't tell us. Go anywhere near the subject and he clams up. Not that I blame him. Pain should be private. It wasn't intended to be a spectator event."

"I know what happened. Susan told me. Do you want to hear it?"

"Of course. I don't mind being a spectator."

It seemed very ordinary, like hackneyed incidents in a vaguely remembered potboiler novel, but clichés can cut and cause emotional bleeding. As my wife unreeled the story, I felt sorry for Frank. It wasn't his fault. All he did was lend his son his truck. Michael's car was on blocks and he and his girlfriend were planning to spend the weekend in Edmonton. Michael shrugged off a radio report that a severe blizzard was surging north. The truck ran out of gas and Michael, four beers in him, tried to cross the highway in swirling snow, bound for a nearby service station. He was struck by a semi and killed. In the family post-mortem conducted by Greg and his mother, Frank was demonized. He let Michael borrow the truck knowing the weather was treacherous. What's more, Frank hadn't fixed the fuel gauge, which tended to stick at empty. Michael obviously figured there was gas in the truck, even though the gauge read otherwise. Already branded a loser by his wife — he wasn't successful like her father — Frank was now even more poorly regarded; in their eyes he was responsible for the death of the family's most charismatic member.

Susan believed blaming Frank for his son's fatal accident was horribly unfair. Michael was half-stewed, Michael should've paid attention to the weather warning, Michael shouldn't have attempted to sprint past the semi. Susan said none of those things to anyone in the family. She adored Greg to such a degree that she gladly granted him ownership of everything she possessed, including her right to voice a contrary opinion.

When the Crumps flew to Nova Scotia for Christmas, Preston seethed with indignant resentment. The couple's three kiddies were courteous and clean, and who liked denying them a holiday with their grandparents, but damnitall, Gordon and Grace Crump shouldn't be enjoying themselves. Welfare paid their rent and put food on their table and it wasn't fair, the government supporting them generously and the family affording to fly.

16

Welfare was a crime to most Prestonites, and the Crumps, the only fit-bodied locals known to be on it, were cruelly scorned. The Nova Scotia flight was a tale that rose, like Marley's ghost, each Christmas for years afterwards. The shunning of the Crumps wasn't, as it may seem, proof positive that live and let live was a concept the town never took to its collective bosom. The shunning was an anomaly; prejudice, in its multiple guises, had lost its potency.

A local dairy farmer discovered this upon proposing at a community centre meeting that the town rescue a Vietnamese family from a squalid refugee camp. Waiting to present the proposition, the farmer chewed his nails. In the late 1940s xenophobia or racism or a made-for-each-other marriage of both obscenities flared when Harry Wong opened the Chinese restaurant on Palliser. Vandals smashed the front window and chalked racial insults on an outer wall, and the Cantonese immigrant was roughed up by town bullies charging he was the pointman for a "yellow" invasion. Wong held his ground and was eventually left alone; his grandson Tommy and his family were now the sole people of Asian ancestry in town, and the farmer fretted over the possibility of community centre members opposing his proposition, masking their racism and xenophobia behind assertions that the rescue would be onerously complex and expensive. To his relief, no one said anything against the scheme and the chairman's call for a vote resulted in a verdict of unanimous approval. The community centre raised funding, and when the Vietnamese family arrived Prestonites donated accommodation, clothing, and English lessons; in due time, the father found a job at the lumber yard.

Not long after the Vietnamese refugees settled in Preston, a black farmer bought three hundred acres of grain-raising land outside town. He was a descendant of the slaves who fled the Civil War to establish a black farming community in the northern Alberta district of Amber Valley. Preston's history was stained by an anti-black episode in the 1930s. A word-of-mouth campaign ignited by a group of businessmen persuaded countless shoppers not to patronize the store a black couple came to Preston to run. When J.J. Maloney, the leader of the provincial Ku Klux Klan, a party that had a bigger following than contemporary Albertans care to admit, spoke at a local hall it was a standing-room-only event. Maloney stated flatly that "the Negro animal" was immoral and mentally sub-normal and should be banned from residing in white areas. In the wake of Maloney's tirade, the store owners were systematically harassed and forced to leave town. Half a century later, the black farmer and his family did not meet with hostile resistance. They became popular figures at barbecues, square dances, auctions, and Frontier Daze festivities. The daughter's contest entries won 4-H ribbons; the son was awarded a university scholarship. "Prejudice? No, I haven't seen none," the farmer told me. "Some old-timers aren't up on the current lingo, but I wouldn't say that's prejudice. I had a laugh at Sunday church. A lady said to me, 'I love Negro spirituals,' and I said, 'We don't use that word anymore.' She frowned and said, 'If you don't use the word spirituals, what do you call them?'"

The town florist wasn't a popular figure in Preston. He swam along with the Frontier Daze tide — Garry's Flower Shop was turned into the Boot Hill Posy Pasture — but he failed to attend barbecues, square dances, and auctions. The florist was gay. There had to be plenty of homosexuals in the town (a national survey claimed that one in every ten Canadians was homosexual), but Garry was the sole Prestonite to burst out of the closet into the klieg-light glare of public opinion. He had a wicked sense of humour, ridiculing himself and his lonely existence as a "farm-land faggot." Gilbert and Sullivan operettas were his passion, and he skipped town events because they bored him. "When everyone dresses in costumes and sings *The Pirates of Penzance,* I'll go to the Sunnyside auction." Reared in Preston, Garry was taunted with homosexual slurs in school, and, striving to fit in, he denied he was gay and feigned an exaggerated lust for girls. When he came out at the age of twenty-three, he was afraid of being assaulted on a downtown street. He wasn't — the town treated him civilly. "I won't go into the Preston Hotel pub for a Saturday night beer," he said, "but there's so many fights in that joint I wouldn't go there if I was heterosexual." Excluding the hotel beer parlour, he felt comfortable anywhere in town. His status paralleled that of the Hutterites. The most critical thing I heard people say about Garry was that, in Hutterite fashion, he kept to himself and didn't socialize.

Preston hadn't eradicated every last fragment of homophobia, racism, and xenophobia, but those attitudes were the treasured values of a minute minority that had no more influence on the town's general course of action than ripples on the Mackenzie River. The news media and entertainment industry engineered the transformation. The liberalization spawned in the 1960s seeped, drop by drop, through the layers of archaic bigotry. A Preston store proprietor said it was the murder of four children in the Alabama church bombing that taught her racism was insidious; a municipal clerk said a Rod Stewart ballad, *The Killing of Georgie,* altered his perspective on gays. The quiet transformation hadn't, I ventured, just taken place in Preston but in other rural enclaves, belying the urban contention that small-town Canada treated social change as though it were a social stigma.

back
roads
*Ted
Ferguson*

17

Jessie's father was ill and, like the chlorine gas that harmed him, the illness was invisible. He had gone to northern BC to help a friend upgrade the plumbing at a paper mill — a brief resumption of the career he had cast aside. There was a potentially deadly mishap, a swiftly contained chlorine leak, and Joe inhaled a sufficient portion of the odourless substance to damage his lungs. His doctor apprised him that his condition was certain to slowly worsen and that he ought to sue the company for a million dollars. Despising lawyers and the notion of prolonged courtroom combat, Joe agreed to the company's initial proposal, a small settlement, which he thoroughly enjoyed wasting on cabin bashes and bar crawls.

Joe was, by habit, a freewheeling conversationalist. Whether you prodded him or not, and most people didn't, he wasn't afraid to share details of his financial status, his sex life, his shameful escapades when he was, in Bush Speak, drunk as a skunk and feeling no pain. Life-long habits are seldom broken, but Joe did draw the line in his customarily wide-open patter by evading references to his cracked health. Prizing his physical power, and revering it in others, he perceived the injured lungs as an embarrassing weakness, diminishing his masculinity. It was almost as though he was scared that his pals might, if they knew how irrevocably flawed he was, turn on him like mother cats attacking unhealthy newborns.

The ailment was in its early phases, and apart from the odd coughing spell that could be mistaken for the onset of a bad cold, he appeared and sounded excellent, as robust as ever. The morning after he arrived at the midnight hour, banging his horn urgently to awaken us, Joe perched on a kitchen chair — the dogs at his feet, content to be in his company — and paid his live-in girlfriend what was, to him, a compliment all women desired.

"She's got floaters."

"Floaters?" I said. "I don't understand."

"Sinkers and floaters. Some broads take off their bras and their boobs sink to the floor. Others take them off and they float like party balloons. Connie's young. Hers are floaters."

"For God's sake, father ..." Jessie muttered into a pan of frying bacon.

"Did I say something wrong? No, ma'am, I didn't. I'm telling the truth and telling the truth isn't wrong." He popped a can of beer and took prescription pills from the pocket of his denim shirt. When Jessie saw him wash the pills down with a swig of Coors she said, plainly dismayed, "I can't believe I'm seeing this. Prednisone and beer."

"The doctor said it was alright."

"I'm not an idiot, father. There isn't a doctor on earth who'd say that."

"Yeah, well, it's my funeral, I'll do what I want."

"That's right, dad, it's your funeral."

Joe shrugged and swung his eyes over to me. "When do the stores open in Preston? The sooner we get the materials, the sooner we'll get started."

The stores opened at nine. Joe and I made the rounds, picking up plastic pipes and metal clamps for the plumbing, oil for his chainsaw, odds and ends for minor household tasks. In the past there had been times when, going about my business in town, I experienced a profound understanding of the sentiments expressed in Colin Wilson's definitive study of alienation, *The Outsider*. Farmers initiated conversations and, speedily discerning that my knowledge of crops and machinery was minuscule, tended to act as if they were speaking to an adult who wasn't potty-trained. Hardware clerks behaved in a similar vein when I posed questions like, "Do I have to buy a screwdriver or can I just hammer the screws in?" Jablonski's junkyard was the worst place; alienation clung to the air like freezer frost. Jablonski was burly and unkempt, a former Army boxer whose tattoos outnumbered his teeth. Evidently inspired by joyous memories of his ring career, he sporadically beat somebody witless in a tavern fight. His dilapidated trailer-home rotted on a lot congested with dead vehicles. "No dog?" I remarked during my first visit. "I thought all junkyards keep them to discourage thieves."

"I don't need no dog," Jablonski scowled. "Thieves are more terrified of me than a goddamned pitbull."

Dealing with Jablonski, obtaining tires and engine parts for the Black Bobcat, I imagined him peering at me and thinking, I'll take this clueless dork's money, but goddamnit, he ain't from Preston, he ain't one of us.

Joe wasn't from Preston, but he spoke the dialect of the labouring class, in both the technical and social categories. Jablonski discerned the tribal link the moment he and my father-in-law began discussing a faulty part in Joe's camper. Their dialogue was unfathomable to me. "What's your differential?" "Six over twelve, forty-two. The head's a CBA three-two-seven." "I sold my last three-two-seven yesterday, but a Ford maximizer fits." "You sure?" "Yup." "Isn't the Ford maximizer square?" "Right, but I'll slap on a Ralph Kramden adjuster and you'll be whistling Dixie."

Intrigued by each other, the two men lingered between rows of partially eaten cars, inhaling the stimulating aroma of spilled gasoline and automotive oil. Jablonski was a hockey fan and a moonshiner whose vodka was, by his own estimation, one hundred proof. Joe wasn't a sports fan, but he did brew basement beer in his Rain Coast days. Hunting was a mutual love. Jablonski went in for small animals, roaming fields on weekends, shooting rabbits, squirrels, gophers, and crows with a scope-equipped, 12-gauge Winchester. Once, he bagged a fox.

"Everyone and his uncle swears rabbit stew's the best small-critter meal, but they ain't had my squirrel. Jalapeno and a spoonful of chili powder in the pot and you'll cook yourself a tasty dish."

"Speaking of shooting," Joe said, "I've been meaning to tell my son-in-law here that he ought to hang 'No Hunting' signs on his land.'"

"Why? I haven't had hunters on my land."

"Not that you know of. Could be you haven't seen or heard them. In the trees, at a distance, that Toggenburg of yours passes for a deer."

"Flush the toilet!"

Joe was under the house, lying on his back, yelling past support timbers and hardwood flooring. Stationed in the bathroom, Jessie lowered the handle and a burst of water rushed through the plastic pipe leading to the septic tank. There was no leakage. We had achieved a jubilant milestone; our plumbing was modernized, albeit in a fashion urbanites would label unsatisfactorily primitive. Water for the kitchen sink, bathtub, and toilet would continue to be hauled up the slope in plastic containers, Alex's daily chore. Numerous times during the summer one of his parents drove him to the foot of the slope, but in winter he was entirely on his own, dragging a container-laden sled, enduring stinging winds and sub-zero temperatures, groaning and grumbling. I explained to Alex that the well trips were good for him, that they built character. He explained to me that he already had character, but as his weekly allowance was at stake, he planned to go on hauling the water.

Joe crawled out.

"Hunky-dory," he said, brushing dirt off his clothing. "Now we've got to move the water from the well to the house. A generator and underground pipes."

"When Alex finishes his schooling and leaves us we'll do it. He has to earn his allowance somehow, and it's better if it's a chore he dislikes. It builds character."

"Character," Joe chuckled. "I bet that's at the top of every kid's Christmas wish list."

In the kitchen, Joe drank coffee and coached Jessie on the preparation of perogies and cabbage rolls, his dinner request. She had been cooking both for so many years, and with such deftness, that his intervention was akin to coaching Wolfgang Puck on how to slice onions.

"Your café in the Flathead — this is its second year."

"Right. Second year."

"Lots of customers?"

"I wouldn't say lots. We're on a lonely road."

"In two years has a single customer walked into the kitchen and told you how to cook a meal?"

"Why should they? We don't do perogies and cabbage rolls. There's a set menu. Nothing elaborate. Bacon and eggs for breakfast, sandwiches for lunch, and steaks for dinner."

"Steaks? Every night?"

"We don't get busloads of tourists. It's loggers and road crews and hunters. Beef eaters. Beef and beer. A lot of the foreign hunters are German. Real beer hounds. I don't know why — maybe it's because they're depressed about losing the war."

"If there isn't much business, why bother with the café?"

"I meet people, have a beer with them."

"The same thing you did before you opened the café. Only now you're not only drinking with them, you're cooking their meals."

"Connie does the cooking."

"Oh, I see. Floaters cooks and you drink."

"I'm on a disability pension, and that's what pensioners do — drink."

"It's your life, father. I'm just thinking of your health."

"Forget my health. My breathing isn't as bad as it was. My lungs are healing themselves."

Sure they were. New tissue was growing, devouring the blight like a self-repairing tire. I silently scoffed at his preposterous claim, and then it occurred to me that he didn't believe it either. He flung all sorts of strange declarations into conversations to stop people insisting he slow down, alter his habits, act like an infirm person. Envisioning him keeling over and coughing himself to death, I had said we could do without a septic tank and pipes, but that drove him to dig in his heels, arguing that his daughter deserved to be liberated from the winter-outhouse ordeal. Conscious of his rising temper, I shut up and complied.

Joe's physical durability was on my mind again the morning we parked the Black Bobcat on the road to the gate and entered the bush. He was teaching me how to use a chainsaw, weaning me off my reliance on fast-burning deadfall. His Husqvarna was long-bladed and heavy, and, as he intended to cut trees for eight hours, I was concerned that the weight of the saw, the woozy July climate, and the gasoline fumes were a dangerous combination. Compounding the anxiety was my apprehension about handling the saw. I stared at it as if I was confronting an ally capable of sudden betrayal. The memory of the seasoned logger who helped construct the root cellar tugged at me. Wielding a chainsaw was practically second nature to him, yet his physique carried the mark of its treachery, the scar on his left cheek. He called the inch-long gouge the Devil's Kiss. Holding the Husqvarna, ready to yank the starter-cord, I begged the Devil not to schedule a special trip up from Hell for my sake — I exhorted him to plant his chainsaw kisses on some twisted soul who wouldn't mind facing the world glass-eyed and noseless.

"You look nervous," Joe said.

"I am nervous. Chainsaws petrify me."

"Don't let them. Chainsaws are safe as long as you aren't reckless. Quit when you're tired. Tired makes you impatient, and impatient makes you reckless. Guys mangle themselves late in the day, when they're beat and they aren't concentrating 150 percent."

I pulled the cord and, engine shrieking, manoeuvred the speeding blade through a poplar. Knife-and-butter; a near-effortless passage. I limbed the toppled tree, sawed the remains into stove-length pieces, and then shifted to a second tree. There's a trick to convincing timber not to fall backwards and wham you, Joe said. You want to it drop to the north, you saw a v-shaped notch on the south; the weight above the v pulls the tree away from you. Following his recommendation, I applied the v-system to every tree I cut; none of them whammed me.

We spelled each other off. While one of us loaded the sawn

back roads
Ted Ferguson

pieces onto the truck, the other worked the Husqvarna. We took coffee breaks and, at noon, ate chicken salad sandwiches. From time to time, I appraised Joe for signs that the tree-cutting was wearing him down. He coughed and he constantly wiped sweat from his face, but otherwise he seemed to be unaffected. In mid-afternoon, I noticed his coughing spells were increasing and he was moving slower, and, sure enough, ten or fifteen minutes later he laid the saw on the ground and said, "I'm done for today. I'm bushed."

So was I. Bushed, and thankful that all of my body parts were located — unsliced, unblemished — in the venues they were located in when I left the house that morning. If Joe hadn't called it quits, I would have. I was losing my focus, giving it less than 150 percent, and the Devil was hovering.

"Fantastic," I said, surveying the stump-pocked clearing. "It's getting harder for me to find deadfall. I've been going deeper and deeper into the woods."

"You aren't off deadfall yet," Joe said. "This timber won't dry for a while."

"Yes, I know."

"Isn't the Husqvarna a dandy machine?"

"I suppose. It still makes me nervous."

"You'll get used to it. By the end of the week you'll be taking it into the bathroom and shaving with it."

We lugged the saw and the gas can to the truck and drove to the house. Joe swallowed beer and a pill and, for the first time at our place, he went to his camper for a pre-dinner rest. He slept for two and a half hours.

It rained the day my father-in-law departed for the mountains, a precise imitation of wispy Vancouver drizzle. Alex and I said our good-byes at the porch door, and Jessie accompanied him into the yard.

Alex ascended the stairs to his room and Supertramp.

"Thank God, he's gone," Jessie said, walking into the kitchen and shedding her rain jacket. "I can't stand seeing him mixing pills and alcohol. Every night he dives into the rum and forgets he's already taken a pill, and no matter what I say he takes another one. His lungs won't kill him; Prednisone and booze will."

"I'm amazed he doesn't drink while he's working. But then there are alcoholic authors who don't hit the bottle until they're finished writing for the day."

"He said something about you just now."

"About me?"

"He's changed his opinion of you."

"In what way?"

"When I told him we were moving here, he thought you were too soft to live in the bush. You surprised him."

Was that a compliment? Yes, I believed so. Joe was saying, if I interpreted it correctly, that the Defective One had mended his flaws and was now an acceptable son-in-law. Coming from a man whose skills I admired, that was a triumph of Olympian stature for me.

18 Mr. Pacino was proud of his rock garden. I was unaware of that in my younger years, but it flashed into my head, decades down the road, while I was sitting at the kitchen window gazing at the firewood I split and piled in chest-high rows near the goat shed. Mr. Pacino was a cherubic widower whose married children brought him rocks that he spread about his gently inclining back yard. Having a rock garden by no means made him unique. Rock gardens were a staple in Victoria, as ubiquitous as doilies, umbrellas, and bone-china tea cups. Mr. Pacino's version, however, existed outside the perimeters of prevailing conventionality. Disdaining the practice of cultivating plants among the rocks, he painted pictures of daffodils, tulips, and various flowers on the surfaces, establishing a garden independent of seasonal influences. Many Sundays, taking the lane behind Mr. Pacino's house en route to the neighbourhood sandlot, I caught him slouching on a porch chair, rumpled and grizzled, staring into vacant air. When I saw him smiling, and there wasn't anybody on the porch except him, I concluded that his brain was missing a few nuts and bolts.

Now I realized the truth. Mr. Pacino wasn't staring into vacant air, and I was mistaken to judge the queer expression to be a symptom of wobbly sanity. He was looking at his rock gallery, with pride and satisfaction, which was pretty much how I felt viewing the firewood rows. In the city, practising journalism, I wrote sentences on paper that were printed on larger sheets of paper and, rewarded for my disciplined behaviour, I received a slip of number-inscribed paper according me the monetary right to distribute number-inscribed slips of paper to landlords, utility companies, whomever I was financially beholden to. Described in those terms, it was clearly a profoundly senseless way for anyone to pass their allotted time on earth, but along with millions of other profoundly senseless Canadians, I took to it with unwavering passion. I liked nudging my bank balance to climb. I liked providing the material comforts my family appreciated. I liked feeling clever, on top of the game.

Cutting firewood and urban career jousting may appear to be pursuits that have nothing whatsoever to do with each other, but there are discernible resemblances. I liked making the wood-pile lengthen and rise. I liked providing the creature comfort (household heat) that my family appreciated, and although I didn't believe I was being remarkably clever, I did believe I was on top of the game, prepared for winter.

I also took pleasure in observing the firewood rows and recall-ing the low-income neighbourhood I was raised in. People did their own repairs and renovations. It wasn't unusual to walk into a house and find a disassembled washing machine motor on the linoleum floor. Adding an extra room onto a house was a family project stretching over months, and there was perpetually some-one somewhere fixing his car, his lawnmower, a sickly radio. Expertise was taken for granted, as though it were genetically imprinted, and praise was issued sparingly. Mr. Dunn was an exception. Neighbourhood residents were forever telling him and each other that he was a genius. An electrician by trade, Mr. Dunn beautified his modest dwelling with furniture he crafted in his basement workshop. Copying designs he fancied in maga-zine photographs and library books, he turned out exquisite rep-licas of high-dollar items. He made Queen Anne dining room chairs and an Edwardian settee. When he exhausted the fillable space in the house, he switched to boat building and painstak-ingly constructed a twenty-foot sloop in his garage.

In situations where being good with your hands is the norm, there is generally one person who can't get the hang of it. In our neighbourhood, it was me. I couldn't drive a screw in straight. The lid for the pencil box I produced at school, devised to slide open and shut, jammed partway. The Woody Woodpecker knocker I attached to our front door fell apart. Explaining to me how a motor vehicle engine functioned was like explaining hos-pital rules to a maternity ward baby. Contributing to my sense of manual ineptitude, the kid next door, a stumble-footed moron, competently installed rings and wiring in his dad's Pontiac.

I remembered those things while staring out of the kitchen window, and I thought of how I would never have guessed back then that I was capable of surviving anywhere I had to rely more on my hands than my mind. I could build a woodpile, though. I had conquered the technique of lowering an axe rapidly without whacking my body, and, with willpower and soaking sweat, brought forth an object of gratifying size and shape.

One September afternoon, Alex alighted from the school bus with a heavy heart and the genesis of a black eye. A kid in his class — a dinky-brained, large-framed, questionably human specimen named George Svoboda — reckoned his second run at grade six would be a more stimulating experience if he bullied my son. Earlier that week, he Indian-rope-burned Alex's arm and stomped his egg-salad sandwich. Leery of us interfering and contacting Svoboda's parents, Alex kept the abusive episodes to himself. The puffy flesh ringing his eye begged for an explanation, and he hesitantly supplied one. Svoboda swaggered up to him in the school yard and belted him in the face. He did nothing to motivate the punch and allied acts of harassment; Svoboda apparently picked Alex for his freshness and availability — no other bully had laid claim to him.

"Please don't talk to his parents," Alex urged us. "This is between him and me. I can handle George Svoboda. He isn't as tough as he pretends he is."

"I won't talk to his parents," I pledged.

"Is there a kid in your class bigger than Svoboda?" Jessie asked.

"Danny's bigger."

"Do you like him?"

"Yeah, he's nice."

"Befriend Danny and Svoboda will leave you alone."

Was she serious? Kids like Svoboda intimidated everyone, whether they were bigger or not. A warped runt in my grade six home room systematically delighted himself by hitting and booting the class giant. No, befriending Danny wasn't the remedy. Direct action was necessary — a secretive dose of parental interference. When Alex's class was on a school excursion, I motored to Sunnyside. It was roughly one-thirty. I believed that people with lunch-packed stomachs were easier to deal with. At Sunnyside Elementary, order and serenity prevailed. The teacher's voice

back roads
Ted Ferguson

filtering through a closed classroom door was composed and mellifluous, the vacated corridors hushed and tidy. I went by lockers and a trophy case and met a boy exiting the principal's office.

"You looking for Mr. Henderson?"

"Yes."

"He isn't in. He's drinking his lunch."

"Eating his lunch," I corrected.

"No, he's drinking it."

The Wild Rose Hotel rose five stories above Sunnyside's main street. It was a dour, 1930s brown-brick, an establishment the villagers said had seen better days, when, in their hearts they knew it hadn't. The pub door bore a hand-printed warning written by a spelling bee loser, "No Shurts, No Shoes, No Sirvice." Henderson and a farmer in green overalls and a John Deere cap were shooting the breeze at a circular table. The principal was a cinch to identify; he was the patron wearing a suit.

I introduced myself.

"Sit down," Henderson said genially. "Give your feet a vacation."

"All right."

"Clarence," he called to the barman, "pour this pilgrim a brew."

"No thanks," I called. "I can't stay."

"Come on, be friendly. How long does it take to drink a beer?"

"In your case," the farmer said, "ten seconds."

I ordered a beer. Henderson swallowed a mouthful of draft and asked, "So what's your problem?"

"A boy in my son's class is bullying him. He gave Alex a black eye yesterday."

"What's his name?"

"George Svoboda."

"George Svoboda? I wonder if he's related to the Svoboda brothers."

"Davy's son," the farmer said.

"Cement for brains. The Svoboda clan's most notable characteristic."

"Davy and me delivered for Preston Cartage," the farmer said. "Thirty-seven years of age and he counted with his fingers."

"I have sharp kids in my school. Kids who'll be doctors and lawyers and accountants. Tommy Boychuk, in grade four, he's a Mensa candidate. He's skipped three grades. Then there's the George Svobodas. If he's anything like his father and uncle, he's phenomenally dense."

"I know his circumstances," the farmer said. "Slaving on the piss-poor family farm. His dad beats him and his mother's a block of ice."

"It figures," the principal said. "Ask a kid like George Svoboda what he wants to be when he's an adult and don't be shocked if he answers, 'Serial killer.'"

"Man, are you cynical," the farmer chortled.

"I'm not cynical. I'm a realist. Some kids are so witless and barbaric their only chance of being successful is playing in the NHL."

"Who's minding the prison?" The man submitting the question was skeletal and jug-eared. He had wandered through the lobby door and stopped behind the principal's chair.

"The teachers are," Henderson said, pivoting his head to face him. "At the slightest hint of trouble, they have my permission to fire the tear gas."

The man guffawed and squeezed Henderson's shoulder. Then he walked — in bare feet — to a corner table.

"Oh, oh," I said. "No shoes, no service."

"Harvey's exempt," the farmer said. "Clarence married his sister. You know Harvey Thomson?"

"No."

"Barefoot the entire summer. Socks and gumboots in winter. He's a local legend. Won't wear shoes and lives in a cave."

Henderson glanced at his watch. "Gotta go." He drained his glass and said, "I'll tell George Svoboda to stop bullying your son."

"I'd rather you didn't. I promised Alex I wouldn't intervene. If you talk to Svoboda, he might tell my son and I'll have to admit I broke my promise. I don't want my son distrusting me."

back
roads
Ted
Ferguson

"Then I won't tell him."

"I was going to suggest posting a notice on the bulletin board. Students apprehended bullying other students will be suspended."

"Sure, but it'll be futile. A piece of paper won't dissuade anyone. I don't know Svoboda, but I have a hunch he's a boy who'd actually welcome a suspension. Less time he'd be forced to spend in school." The principal stood up and buttoned his suit jacket. "Phone me if you come up with another proposal. I'm always willing to listen to parents."

I didn't call.

Alex befriended Danny and George Svoboda left him alone.

Judith's Chrysler was parked close to the mall entrance, washed and waxed, a suitably spiffy carriage for rural royalty. Her husband did the food shopping, and the instant I saw him in the distant reaches of the supermarket, packed into the double-breasted suit, I suspected she was waiting in the car. Wheeling a grocery cart out of the mall, I nodded and smiled at Judith. She did neither. She turned her head. There were shoppers in the vicinity and, I guessed, she didn't want them to associate her with the owner of a dusty and dented junkyard clunker. Her marriage to Frank notwithstanding, she conducted herself as if the townsfolk were jurists whose opinions dictated the length of her duration on earth; too many negative evaluations and they'd vote for shortening her life span. Judith's qualms about other people's disapproval were so severe they were nearly comical. She forbade Frank, for instance, to set foot inside the liquor store in case a prominent citizen saw him with a bottle and erroneously pegged her as a drinker.

After the mall snubbing, the last thing I expected was for Judith to issue an invitation for our family to attend her birthday dinner. Wasn't she nauseated by the possibility that her neighbours would see our truck in her driveway? What if we didn't dress for the occasion and walked to the door presenting a flesh-and-blood visualization of her favourite term for impoverished locals, "raggedy hillbillies."

"Why is she inviting us?" Jessie pondered.

"I wish I knew," I said. "It isn't because she enjoys our company."

"Let's not go."

"Fine with me. I'll say I've got a story deadline."

Susan came by the house. She loved her mother-in-law dearly, she said (unconvincingly), but the annual dinner was an ordeal. Greg was so uptight he scarcely spoke, and with his wife in the room, Frank reined in his conversation and was cap-in-hand

20

servile. Each time Susan opened her mouth, she did it with trep-
idation, praying she wouldn't inadvertently offend Judith. She
implored us to go, to give her someone to talk to, and for her
sake we agreed.

Judith had no neighbours. To get to her place, we rode along
Preston's main drag and veered onto a road that penetrated
the town's slowly expanding subdivision. Judith's house was on
the prairie, a sombre Victorian redbrick surrounded by a wind-
cutting hedge. Greg's Mustang was parked on the gravel, behind
the maroon Chrysler. We went to the door feeling well-prepared.
Scrubbed skin, clean hair, smart clothing.

"This isn't necessary," Frank said, receiving our birthday
gift — a six-pack, wrapped in cheery paper, of the English mar-
malade Judith purportedly spread on breakfast toast. "She'd be
content with a card. A Hallmark with a blissful verse."

His wide chest was encased in a rumpled denim shirt, nibbled
at the collar and cuffs, and I speculated that he had committed
a startling deed of defiance and refused to don the grey suit for
his wife's birthday.

He escorted us to the kitchen.

Greg and Susan were drinking coffee at an Arborite table.
Susan had touched her face lightly with lipstick, forsaken mas-
cara, and muted her breasts, an urgent voice most of her waking
hours, with a dowdy, loose-fitting dress. Greg's shirt and slacks
were meticulously ironed, his hair untypically neat. His mother
wasn't hanging over him, a dark, critical force, but he clearly
sensed she was. He had the appearance of a patient scheduled for
surgery in a hospital that had run out of anaesthetics.

"Can I watch TV?" Alex asked.

"You bet," Frank replied. "It's in the parlour. Keep the sound
low. Don't crank it above the mark on the cabinet."

"Mark?"

"Blue ink. Anything above it's loud for my wife."

"Okay."

"You folks want coffee?"

"No, thanks," Jessie and I answered simultaneously.

I scanned the Moffat stove. No pots on the elements and the oven light was off. What was going on? Wasn't it a family custom for Judith to cook the birthday meal, and in exchange, for Susan to cook the Christmas turkey? And where was Judith — sprucing up for the celebration?

"I'm surprised the goats aren't with you," Susan teased. "I thought the four of you can't bear to be parted."

"We can bear to be parted from them but they can't stand being parted from us," Jessie said. "They'd climb into the bathtub with us if we let them."

"When I go for a walk, Jessie tethers the goats till I disappear. Lately, they're braver. When we take the truck up our road, they gallop after it. They panic and gallop to the house if we drive off the property."

"Someday they won't gallop to the house," Susan said. "You'll be in Edmonton, shopping at Eaton's, and the goats will be on the escalator right behind you."

"I don't care," Jessie said, "as long as they sweep up their own turds. I'd be embarrassed to do it in public."

"Did you find them winter feed?" Frank asked me.

"Yes. Remember the guy whose field we crossed the day we moved the house? He's selling us hay. Next spring he'll plant oats on our field and we'll share the crop."

"How many bales for you?"

"Two or three hundred, depending on the size of the crop. He says the goats will go through a bale a day."

"Not a bad deal. There'll be leftovers for their bedding."

The door bell rang and Frank went to answer it.

"Where's your mother?" I asked Greg.

"She's lying down," he said quietly.

"She's not just lying down," Susan said. "When we got here, Frank said Judith isn't feeling well and will probably be in bed for a few days."

"The flu?"

"Maybe. He didn't say."

Frank returned clutching a pizza box.

"Everybody hungry? Drag your boy away from the television. We'll be classy and eat in the dining room."

I went into the parlour to retrieve Alex. He was watching a Donald Duck cartoon, a lowering of standards for a Marvel comics reader. With no television at home, everything on the tube was engrossing to him.

Surveying the parlour, it struck me that the room was pleasantly decorated, in a sort of top-of-the-line discount warehouse style. Going into the dining room, I noted that it was equally as pleasant, equally as yawningly noncommittal. Where were the distinctive items reflecting the occupants' personality: the family pictures, the holiday mementos, the chenille throw, the *Hogan's Heroes* portrait they couldn't resist in the Esso parking lot? They had to be somewhere; Judith seldom left the house and people who seldom left their house found life intolerable without the comforting presence of objects conveying a special meaning. The bedroom, I decided. Judith's special objects covered the walls and cluttered the carpet in the refuge she retreated to with such consistency.

"The pizza's swell, isn't it?" Frank said, soliciting expressions of gratitude to pass on to Judith, who footed the bill for the meal.

"It's a winner," Susan said (again unconvincingly).

I said nothing. The thick, rubbery crust, canned ham and pineapple, and sweet, unidentifiable coating comprised the worst pizza I ever tasted. I was grateful, nonetheless. Grateful that due to Judith's penny-pinching nature, I only had one slice to consume.

"You need a phone," Frank said to Susan. "I could've called and told you Judith wasn't up to a birthday supper. You'd have been saved the trip to town."

"We don't want a phone," Susan said, sounding as though she had been repeating that position, uttering those very words, for years.

"I don't understand why not."

"We've no one to call. We don't know anybody in town."

"You know Judith and me. We'd be in touch more."

"I wouldn't mind a telephone," Jessie said, helping Susan wriggle off Frank's hook. "I worry when Ted's off someplace and I hear there's a blizzard."

"You're quite a ways from the highway cable," Frank said. "The phone company won't be eager to string it to your land. Dollars to doughnuts, the manager will stall by writing your name at the bottom of a list. He'll stall two or three years and hope you'll move before he has to send a crew in."

"No problem," I said. "We're not in a hurry. The reason we haven't applied is it will cost us a fortune, stringing the cable that distance."

"Who told you that?"

"A woman in the laundromat."

"Whoever she was, she was jerking your chain. In Alberta it's free, no matter what the mileage is. Listen, why don't I fix it so you won't be on the bottom of the list?"

"How?"

"Never mind how. We'll trade. A sack of carrots when your garden's dug, and I'll guarantee you a phone by winter." .

Frank had cancelled the birthday cake, substituting a small box of butter tarts. I almost trembled at the thought of following the hideous pizza with a sugar-saturated dessert.

"None for me, thank you. I'm full."

"You're denying yourself a genuine treat. The mall bake shop's a treasure. Folks drive from Sunnyside and McWhirter and all over for their butter tarts."

"For crying out loud, father," Greg growled, "you've told him that six million times since he landed in Alberta."

"Doesn't make it less true. You know, Greg, you ought to take your visitors there. When are they due?"

"In two weeks," Greg said.

Visitors? Were Susan's parents coming?

No, Susan said. Friends. Mark and Teri Kelly.

Mark was a law student, the prodigy of a ritzy Vancouver family. He wandered the planet for six years before settling in Kitsilano and submitting to his father's desire that he enter UBC and "make something of himself." Teri was an ex-department store clerk reared on cheeseburgers and ham sandwiches her waitress mom snuck out of the greasy spoon. An unlikely union of contrasting enclaves; South Marine Drive marrying Sam and Rosie's Magic Meadows Trailer Park. During the wedding ceremony, both of Mark's parents cried. His mom because she was losing her son, his dad because he was losing that son to a trailer-trash Untouchable.

Despite his snobby background, Mark was down-to-earth, a guy you could talk to. Teri wasn't as bright as her husband, but she was gentle and nice, very feminine.

Real good people, Susan purred, and she loved them madly.

] "Well, that was baffling," Jessie said in the truck.

"Yeah, but it couldn't have been important. If it was, Frank would've mentioned why we were invited."

"I don't mean Judith. I mean Susan and her visitors. She said one thing and her eyes said another."

"I picked up on that. The Kellys are a golden couple and she loves them, but she didn't look pleased to be seeing them again."

"Apprehensive. That's how she looked to me. Like the landlord's coming and she can't pay the rent."

The Dunes were off the beaten track, a scratch of geological strangeness on the Prairies' immense body, yet somehow their reputation as cheap land leaked into civilization far removed from northern Alberta. Every once in a while, a latter-day misfit strutted into the woods vowing to establish a personal kingdom. In other words, the dreamers, ne'er-do-wells, and self-deluding social outcasts hardly anybody wanted came to the land hardly anybody wanted.

21

A few succeeded, most didn't.

Unwittingly emulating the Vikings who once explored Canada, some failing Dunes settlers left behind traces of their temporary foothold. Past Mirror Lake, on the cusp of a spruce-studded clearing, lay the crumbling foundation for a house that was never erected. Elsewhere in the Dunes, a flat-tired bailer rusted within the shadow of an abandoned shack joined to the unfinished frame of a rear-room extension.

If I failed and limped back to the city, I could draw a modest ration of solace from the realization that, unlike many defeated settlers, I had completed my building projects. For a long while that sense of achievement dangled beyond my reach. I was building a garage, the last outdoor carpentry job on my agenda, and I was labouring on it in summer, when the woods were green and lavish and wind gusts transmitted whiffs of pine from the ravine at the end of the municipal road. Walking in the forest was such a compelling event that I chose to do that before stopping at the garage site where, weary and hankering for dinner, I did barely enough work to assure myself the project was progressing. As it wasn't an essential task — we had survived three winters without a garage — I often suspended work on it for weeks.

The garage was, of course, designed to accommodate the truck. In winter I'd stash the battery behind the stove, sled it to the front gate and, on marrow-freezing days, sprawl on the snow-laden ground to heat the engine block with a propane torch. The garage was intended to eliminate the snow-laden ground torment and the necessity of digging the truck out from under blizzard dumpings. But while I was working on the garage, the Black Bobcat developed a trait that led me to decide it would never occupy the enclosure. It turned into a mobile distribution centre for mechanical aggravation. The fan belt broke one week; the brake linings had to be replaced the next. The muffler detached itself on Palliser Street; both headlights expired during a late night journey.

The morning that the gear shift began to spring out of second, I had Jablonski install a reconditioned transmission and then I travelled to Edmonton to secure a factory-fresh vehicle Frank said was the epitome of low-priced, automotive reliability. The Honda Civic lacked the Black Bobcat's scruffy individualism. Alex scrutinized the bland, pale-green chassis and pronounced the car too dull to tag with a nick-name. "Hondas are for old people," he protested. "My science teacher's mother drives a Civic. So does that ninety-year-old guy in Sunnyside who forgets to do up his zipper." Discarding my son's plea not to assign his beloved truck a downgraded role, I resolved to anchor it in the yard for the winter and, in hotter weather, fire it up solely for workhorse missions, such as fetching well water and firewood blocks.

The garage nestled at the side of our road, several yards inside the gate. The design was basic and crude, in accordance with my status as a know-nothing carpenter. Designating four poplars as posts, I sawed the tops off at the six-foot level and built the walls by nailing thinner poplars between them. The trees were uneven and there were gaps in the walls, but I figured the amount of snow blowing into the garage wasn't worth fretting over. When the walls were finally standing, I planned to build a particle board roof and cover the entrance with a tarpaulin.

One afternoon, I was gazing at a waist-high wall and wondering if I had bent so many nails banging them in that they didn't sink deep enough to maintain a stable hold. I heard a noise in the woods, like a large animal advancing across the Crown quarter, and, gaping down the road to the house, I prayed it wasn't a bear with a grudge against humankind. A burly, spade-bearded man materialized at the barbed wire fence. He parted the strands and, disregarding the signs I had posted — "No Trespassing," "Private Property," "No Hunting"— he stepped onto the road.

"Hey, what are you doing?" I called out.

The man acted as if I wasn't there. He reached under the bottom strand to retrieve a scope-mounted rifle, and then started walking in the opposite direction.

"You can't hunt here," I declared.

He halted and turned. "What's it to you?"

"People live here."

"I won't shoot them."

"We have goats."

"I won't shoot them either."

"I'm sorry, you'll have to go somewhere else."

"You booting me off your property?"

"You shouldn't be hunting, anyway. The season's closed."

"Hold on, buddy. Don't lecture me on when I can and can't shoot deer."

"I'm not lecturing. Hunt whenever you want — I'm just asking you not to do it on my land."

He stood rock-still and glared, as if he was debating whether mine were the kind of face he'd enjoy stomping. My stomach weakened and the nape of my neck hardened. Faking an expression of invincibility, I struggled to root my feet to the earth for several month-long moments. It was not, I told myself, a good idea to try to escape a battering by lecturing him about violence being a childish way to settle a dispute. Relief flowed, a gigantic wave, when he moved to the fence and vanished through the barbed wire.

back
roads
*Ted
Ferguson*

22

My mother used to caution me that there were individuals among us who could charm the birds out of the trees. Vacuum cleaner salesmen, insurance agents, and politicians were the worst examples, and if I knew what was best for me when I grew up, I would steer clear of all of them. Mark Kelly didn't belong to any of those professions, but he did fit my mother's description. He was a bird-charmer who was so enthralled by his own talent for telling engaging stories that he seemed to listen intently to whatever you said, scouting for a chance to insert an anecdote.

"Where were you in Mexico? Acapulco?"

"No, San Miguel de Allende."

·"I was heading to Acapulco and I got mugged in Tijuana. I wound up announcing for an evangelical station in Texas. I was on the midnight-to-six shift, playing the Osmond Brothers and Elvis's gospel songs and reading attention-grabbers like the Twenty-Third Psalm. Between records, I'd beg for donations and mail sacred gifts to listeners contributing a hundred dollars. The garbage religious nuts digest is mind-boggling. In the first month, I mailed two-hundred and fourteen-hundred dollar donors autographed pictures — of Jesus Christ!"

Mark's anecdotes didn't necessarily lead to humorous punchlines. Some were shocking, some angry, some poignantly tragic. The unanswerable question was, did all or any of the incidents he related actually happen to him or was he a highly proficient story thief, appropriating them from multiple sources? The answerable question was, did it matter to me? No, it didn't. He was entertaining, he was compassionate, he was obliging, and I liked him. However, even though I wasn't following my mother's advice and according Mark a wide berth, I did warn myself against putting credence in his word on anything vital, like a can't-lose investment.

While Mark's personality sprang forth clear and bold the first night I met him at Greg and Susan's, his wife's did not. Teri sank into the couch, leaning sideways to point inaudible comments into Susan's ear when she wasn't smiling at Mark or flicking nervous eyes between Jessie and me, presumably assessing whether or not it was safe to expose her convictions, her inner self. My mother periodically said that still waters ran deep, but the second time we joined the Kellys at Greg and Susan's, Teri removed her muzzle, scattering opinions helter-skelter and reminding me that still waters also ran shallow.

So if it wasn't shared intellect that brought the couple together, what was it?

Discourse.

Mark was an average-looking guy, someone women looked at on the street with the same degree of wanton desire they displayed looking at lampposts. When he saw Teri, a diminutive, sloe-eyed beauty clerking at Woodward's, he was immediately smitten. He returned to the department store three times to ask her for a date, and twice she said no. She capitulated the day he stated that he was studying law and he was anxious to take her to an elegant restaurant, The Three Greenhorns. She hadn't dated anybody who had been on a university campus, apart from a lawn mower operator, and she hadn't eaten in a place that didn't scorn flip-flops and cut-offs so she thought, Why not, I'll tell him, very politely, to get lost after he drives me home.

For all of the mass media theorizing that women strip their bodies and souls naked for muscular pretty-boys, in truth they rated physical perfection secondary to verbal bonding. Mark instinctively divined how to speak to Teri: when to sympathize, when to praise, when to counsel, and, perhaps the most crucial element, when to clam up and listen. After the dinner, they lounged in Teri's apartment, chatting the hours away until 4 AM.

Guys usually acted like they were fascinated by Teri, Susan said, but the only part of them genuinely fascinated hung below their belts. Mark sincerely cared about everything Teri said and did, and women fall for men who sincerely care about everything they say and do.

back
roads
*Ted
Ferguson*

1 We were taking Mark to the Sunnyside auction, the three of us cramming the front seat of the Black Bobcat. He lowered his window to breathe cool air and sweep curious eyes over the houses and barns and crop-crowded fields dimming under an overcast sky and stretching twilight.

"Television killed the movie theatres in Prairie towns," he said. "I'm amazed the auction halls survived."

"Television was responsible for a lot of Prairie traditions falling by the wayside," I said. "Community quilting bees have more or less disappeared."

"It's incredible," Jessie said. "Farmers enjoy the auctions so much they go in the crummiest weather. Freezing cold, dust storms; hail the size of oranges doesn't deter them. Pouring rain — and a cyclone tears the roof off the hall — they'd probably grab a raincoat and go."

"What's the strangest thing you've seen on the auction block?"

"The strangest?" I said. "That's a tough question. I imagine it was the stuffed cat."

"It wasn't the fact that somebody was selling it that was strange," Jessie said. "It was the fact that somebody actually bought it."

"Was the cat mummified?" Mark queried.

"Mummified? No, I don't think so," I replied.

"There are mummies in Japan. The Japanese hide them from Westerners, but a friend teaching in Sakata said I could see one in a mountain temple. The first cabbie I asked to drive me there seized up. He insisted the temple didn't exist. The second cabbie I asked said he'd take me, he wasn't a Buddhist. The mummy was eerie. A tiny, shrunken monk propped upright in a glass showcase, the identical position he died in thousands of years ago. He had dug a hole on the temple grounds, sat in it and starved himself to death. He was considered an extraordinary figure because he died on the day he predicted, the anniversary of a major event on the Buddhist calendar."

We reached the Sunnyside turn-off.

The auction wasn't scheduled to begin for another hour. It was a fundamental rule to arrive early, I told Mark, and thoroughly inspect the items that appealed to you. Otherwise, you might purchase damaged goods or an article that looked better from the floor than it did in your hand. I had adopted the early-bird custom, I explained, in the wake of two unfortunate acquisitions: a 1930s coffee pot riddled with minuscule holes and an amateur artist's copy of a Gainsborough portrait that, at a distance, I mistook for an authentic masterpiece that had, by a spin of mischievous fate, landed on a bankrupt farm.

"Stand close to Jessie and me so we won't bid against each other," I said.

"Will do. Anything else?"

"Feign indifference," Jessie said. "Look excited and people will think you're onto something valuable and they'll bid the price up."

"And don't react to the auctioneer's opening number. He may be casting a high price over the gathering; if no one bites, he'll drop it."

"What else?"

"Nothing I can think of at the moment."

"So be it," Mark said. "Let the games begin."

The Sunnyside auction was as much a social event as it was a sale. Farm wives grouped at the edges of the big, stuffy, low-ceilinged former Legion hall to eat hot dogs and catch up on community news, while old-timers assembled on metal folding chairs, never bidding, wagging their heads and whispering whenever an object they would've burned in a backyard fire fetched a handsome amount. A dog rummaged the floor for scraps; children searched for empty pop bottles to return for the deposits at the confection booth. The auctioneer, a string bean in a purple Stetson, shimmery velveteen shirt and cowboy boots, was an accomplished purveyor of cornball humour; laughter coursed through the audience when he held up a wooden toilet seat and asked, "Who'll start the bidding on this gorgeous picture frame?"

Mark was entranced. Forgetting my advice, he drifted loose from us. He was all over the room, talking to everyone: farmers, their wives, the town mayor, the town drunk. He bought a bag of potato chips and shared it with the scrounging dog. He scored two or three pocket-sized items and in the heat of the moment he raised his hand when he was already the highest bidder. Minutes later, realizing he was bidding on a slag-glass lamp set we coveted, Jessie lowered her arm.

"I loved the auction," Mark said, carrying the lamp to the truck.

"I thought you would," I said.

"Do you go every week?"

"Not anymore. We did when we were furnishing our house."

"We went everywhere," Jessie said. "Some of the sales were in backwaters where the locals treated you like the last outsider they saw was an encyclopedia salesman in 1929."

"You guys must know everything there is to know about auctions."

Not really. But we did have memorable experiences, good and bad.

One summer we drove 150 miles to a farm sale in response to a poster tacked to the laudromat notice board saying Granny McGregor was leaving her homestead for Saskatoon and she was shedding her possessions, which encompassed numerous antiques. We envisaged a bent-spined old lady and a weather-worn frame house. Granny, an energetic, sharply garbed school teacher, was a member of the mob milling about in front of a recently stuccoed duplex. She informed us that the electrical appliances, the leather couch and the bedroom suite were hers; the sealers, primitive tools, and nineteenth-century furniture over by the original homestead — a collapsed log house — were transported from neighbouring farms by a cunning auctioneer plotting to lure antique seekers to his isolated territory. The seventeen-dollar Pathe gramophone turned it into a worthwhile trip for us. I doubted the fellow gaining the spinning wheel the auctioneer said was hand-crafted in the 1800s was equally as satisfied; the spinning wheel was made of plywood.

I didn't see any of the Sunnyside regulars at Granny McGregor's, and I didn't see Kirk Swanson, an eccentric auction addict known from the Foothills to the Manitoba border. Swanson specialized in crap. Chipped pottery, curtain rods, moth-chewed rugs, enamel sinks, flotsam and jetsam one step short of the local dump. Auctioneers cherished Swanson. He snapped up the junk nobody bid for, taking it to a farm south of Red Deer where it served no purpose except helping fill a crap-clotted barn. The auctioneers cherished Derek Mortimer, too. The antique dealer's appearance at a country sale guaranteed steeper prices, for he consistently out-bid the locals on furniture he peddled for inflated sums in his Edmonton shop. We lost bidding duels with Mortimer, but there were victories. He overlooked a seventy-year-old sideboard that had its natural elegance concealed by layers of white paint. We got it for twenty dollars, scraped the paint off, and applied linseed oil to the oak surface. The sideboard was a gem; it contained a rolltop cupboard and a built-in flour sifter. Once, and only once, I out-bid Mortimer. We both wanted a floral-patterned Victorian settee; I obtained it for one hundred dollars, a bargain price considering I had seen an identical piece going for three times that amount in a Montreal antique store.

Travelling the northlands, we discovered that the auctioneers were, like the goods on the block, a mixed assortment. Some were exceptionally serious, von Karajans conducting Prokofiev symphonies, while others were sullen and testy, accusing non-responsive crowds of being a pack of tight-fisted cheapskates. The clowns in the profession donned dresses they were selling or pretended to cut their assistant's hair with garden shears.

"The farmers invariably laugh," I said to Mark. "So many negative things happen to them — mediocre crops, winter isolation, whatever — their minds are screaming for the slightest hint of humour. I could be wrong, but it seems to me that after they take their crops to the grain elevator and hear how little they're being paid is the time they laugh the hardest at the auctioneer's silly jokes.

back
roads
Ted
Ferguson

It was true, as Mark stated, that television rang the death knell for the small-town movie houses dotting the Prairies, but it was also true that at least one proprietor heard the ringing and plugged his ears. Mike Evanko opened the Dreamland on Pallister Street in 1954 and, despite the cathode creature's deep-slashing impact on attendance numbers, he frequently said he'd close the theatre the day the undertaker closed the lid on him.

Evanko and his wife lived in a tiny suite opposite the projection booth. They ate skimpy meals, quit smoking, and siphoned their modest retirement savings to aid in the financing of the Dreamland's survival. Wherever the cash infusion went, it wasn't spent on restoration. The exterior masonry was gnawed; the neon above the marquee was kept dark because it read Drmlnd. The lobby carpeting was stained, theatre seats bumpy and frayed. The washrooms were fine, save for the nauseating over-abundance of cleaning fluid. They smelled as if the town sadist stapled Glad air-fresheners inside your nostrils. Evanko and his wife were in their seventies, stooped and wobbly, crumbling like the building. While she hunched in the ticket booth, dreaming of block-long line-ups, he made popcorn in the antiquated lobby machine. The popcorn was free and the night a Burt Reynolds twin bill attracted an unusually big crowd (twenty-eight people) Evanko's bliss encouraged him to bestow second bags during intermission.

Aiming to swell the overall attendance, Evanko initiated Bingo Wednesdays and Door-Prize Fridays. Both flopped. Played between films during double bills, Dreamland Bingo awarded winners free movie tickets, whereas the relentlessly popular Legion Bingo, also held on Wednesdays, awarded contestants varying amounts of cash. The only two competitors in the audience for the launching of Door-Prize Friday — movie tickets and a tin of biscuits — were husband and wife. The Saturday afternoon Cartoon Festival was Evanko's final stab at boosting patronage with a special event.

All but a few parents banned their kids from going; the wary majority felt the Dreamland was crawling with lice and fleas and, it wouldn't astound them, cholera and yellow fever germs. A rumour flamed their anxiety; the story that a child's hair fell out in clumps after a diseased Dreamland cat clawed her ankle.

"How many cats do you have?" I asked Evanko one evening.

"Four."

"Are the mice that bad?"

"Not mice," he deadpanned. "Rattlesnakes."

The flash of wit was an anomaly. Evanko was generally a stern and judgmental soul, serviceable traits for an individual devoted to tracking examples of celluloid misconduct. He pre-screened the films and, encountering offensive material, substituted a classic from his bootleg private stock: a Marx Brothers romp or a Frank Capra fantasy. Lippy children and unhygienic motorcyclists were causes for dismissal. Movies depicting drag racing and movies featuring Australian actors (an Aussie hitch-hiker robbed him in 1937) were automatically repelled. Men could bare their chests but if a woman did it she'd better be breast-feeding a baby. When *Saturday Night Fever* reached the Dreamland, Evanko skipped the pre-screening process; Hollywood musicals were, it went without saying, moralistic fairytales. John Travolta's gutter language and lust-inspiring dancing appalled him. He stopped the film and refunded the admission price to furious audience members, principally teenage boys and, they crossed their fingers and prayed, their lust-inspired girlfriends. Evanko branded Travolta a dishonourable dispenser of cinematic filth and summarily passed up subsequent pictures he appeared in.

By virtue of Evanko's quirky intolerance, old movies hugely out-numbered the new. Old or new, Evanko tended to schedule flicks from matching genres. A war double bill, a romance double bill, a western double bill, and so on. Periodically, he linked movies based upon their titles: *Showboat* and *Ship of Fools, White Christmas* and *The Blue Dahlia, The Last Time I Saw Paris* and *Massacre in Rome, The Cocoanuts* and *Bananas*. The citizenry hungered

back
roads
Ted
Ferguson

for Mel Gibson and breast-baring Jane Fonda — Evanko fed them Van Johnson and Kathryn Grayson.

Evanko denied the Dreamland fare was a factor in the theatre's shortage of popularity. He blamed television ("small screen for small brains"), the subdued street lighting ("people don't see us and remember we're here"), and the younger generation's vapid mentality ("all the boys care about is hockey and girls, and all the girls care about is boys"). The Dreamland had its regulars. The projectionist's wife and the cleaning lady, admitted without charge, turned up weekly. Three widows tired of singalongs and gin rummy fled the Prairie Vista senior citizens' lodge together to sit in a middle row. An intense youth aspiring to direct films slouched in the front row with a pen-sized flashlight, writing in notebooks.

Some nights nobody came.

Evanko made popcorn, his wife hunched in the booth, and no one tramping along the near-deserted street, one block south of the near-deserted town core, had halted to buy a ticket. Jessie alleged Evanko shut the theatre early on those nights and took himself upstairs to engage in the guilty pleasure of watching television. I disputed that. The Dreamland was open until the last scene of the last reel was screened. I pictured Evanko camping behind the confectionery counter, staring in optimistic anticipation at the entrance door, while inside the empty theatre the projection light flickered and Bing Crosby sang *Count Your Blessings* to the cats.

Greg was in the lake, up to his waist, rubbing shampoo into his shaggy, wet hair.

"Come in, you guys," he prodded. "It's great."

"Too cold for me," Teri said.

"It's warm — once you get used to it." "Oh, yeah," Susan told Teri. "That's what they say about the Arctic Ocean."

The chilly water failed to discourage Mark. He was in the middle the lake, speeding towards the opposite shore. A high school freestyle medalist, he was apt to swim a mile or two before joining us for a picnic lunch. I never learned how to swim, but I did learn how to wade, and sooner or later, my body demanding relief from the baking hotness, I would change into my bathing suit and languish among the lily pads. I wasn't keen on wading at that moment; I was keen on looking at Teri. Jessie and Alex were at home, summer flu companions, and, waiting for Mark and Greg to leave the water, I reclined on a picnic blanket, inspected Teri's delicate face, and pondered a question that all men ponder at some point in their life: how could a woman so enchanting to look at be so boring to listen to?

"Your cooler's neat," Teri said. "It's bigger than ours. Where'd you get it?"

"Canadian Tire," Susan answered.

"Oh, no, not Canadian Tire. A bunch of retards. Mark sent me to their stupid store to buy an extinguisher for our apartment. The kind you hang by the stove for a grease fire or something. So I go to the mall and this Guido's blocking the aisle with a cart. He's got on a store jacket and I can't see his gold necklace, but I know he's a Guido because of the Eyetie nose and slicked hair. So I ask him where the fire extinguishers are and he says, 'Aisle nine.' I go to aisle nine and there's no extinguishers. So I go to the desk and ask this dumb blonde and she says, 'Aisle twenty-nine.' I drag myself all the way to twenty-nine and the

24

back roads
Ted Ferguson

extinguishers are there, like she said. I buy one and lug it to the apartment and screw it on the wall and then Mark cruises in at six-thirty, gawks at it, and goes, 'This is no good, the gauge says recharge.' I go, 'It can't be no-good, I just got it.' And he goes, 'See for yourself, pet. The gauge is on red. Recharge. It should be straight up and down, where it says full.' I practically threw a conniption — marched into the store first thing the next morning and gave them holy shit. Retards. They should've known it was a dud. I won't set foot in a Canadian Tire store. Not if the company president crawls on his knees and begs me."

"Clerks will sell you anything these days," Susan said. "I count my change, too. The cash register tells them how much they owe you and they still get it wrong."

"Bloody awful," Greg contributed from the water. "It's like their bodies are there but their heads are on coffee break."

"How the hell would you know?" Susan exploded. "You don't shop, I do it all for you!"

Greg's face darkened. He glowered, he blinked, and then, typically Greg, he slid into the water and swam away. I rolled onto my back, gazed at the sky and deemed Susan's razor-slash quite logical. She adored her husband to a point just short of idolization, but it was clear to me she was among the millions of women who, frustrated by the male animal's persistent imperfections, blew their cork from time to time. (If Jesus had married, His wife probably would have berated Him for hanging out with twelve of His best buddies and not staying home at night.) It was woman's nature to desire marital perfection, man's nature to disappoint her. If Susan did become disappointed with Greg every now and then, she hadn't, as far as I knew, blown up or criticized him in the presence of other people.

"You're so good to him," Teri said. "I'm sure he appreciates it."

"He says he does, but I'm skeptical."

"Mark's a sweetie pie. He brings me chocolates and flowers. Thank-you gifts for making his meals."

"Greg doesn't give anyone presents except his mother. He bends over backwards for her. No, that's not right. He orders me to bend over backwards for her. His mother hinted she'd like a hot water bottle for Christmas and I had to drive to the city to get one."

"A hot water bottle? How screwy, wanting that for Christmas."

"It isn't screwy if you know Judith Tyson. She hints at what she'd like to receive so she won't have to spend money on it herself. Greg gave her a toothbrush holder for her birthday last year. And a toothbrush because she hinted hers was in rotten shape. It's insane. Greg goes out of his way — or makes me go out of my way — to please her, and she never gives us presents."

"Me, I'm always good to Mark's mother, and I can't stand her. She's a rich bitch endlessly harping about the plight of dirty slum kids and the whales in the Stanley Park aquarium. She's a wreck. She cries reading hard-luck stories in the newspaper. But she's easier to take than his dad. Mister Bigshot. He acts like the whole world ought to kowtow to him. He'll go ballistic when Mark tells him he's kissing law school good-bye."

"Maybe he'll persuade Mark to change his mind."

"Mission impossible. Mark's sworn a blood oath not to cave in to his father again."

"I didn't know Mark was quitting law school," I interjected. "What's he planning on doing?"

"We're moving here. We're flying to Vancouver next week and cleaning out our apartment."

"I had no idea Alberta appealed to you so much."

"It's beautiful here. We're going to find a house and grow veggies and raise chickens and be real, honest-to-goodness farmers."

They were in no hurry to find that house.

Judith had granted the Kellys permission to move into the lodge for an indefinite period.

I listened in awe as Susan described how Mark had gone to Preston alone, shared a pot of tea with Judith at the dining room table and, smoothly, cannily, convinced her to do what she had balked at doing for Susan's parents when they visited their daughter, let them bed down amid her father's spic and span residue. How did Mark pull it off? Introduced to Judith at Greg and Susan's, he noted she was impressed when Susan said he was a law student and his father was a senior partner in a giant firm. Moments later, her snobbery surfaced. She eulogized her dead father, stressing his importance as a community builder, and she mentioned her extensive real estate holdings. At her house in Preston, Mark played up to Judith's snobbishness by inferring that the two of them were members of a superior class. He twisted the truth substantially, claiming he was taking a sabbatical. By the time he was finished sucking up to Judith, she felt honoured to provide accommodation for such an educated boy from such a distinguished family.

Teri was glad about the lodge, but she said she was itching to have a place to call her own. A huge, rambling, old farmhouse she'd jam to the rafters with kids. With no brothers and sisters, a deserter father, and a working mother, she was lonely growing up and yearned for a big family, children to love and be loved by. How could they afford it, the house and kids, with neither of them employed? Money wasn't a hindrance. Mark's grandmother died and left him a few bucks.

After the picnic, I went home and passed the news on to Jessie. She took it all in and then, quoting a bad line from a bad war movie, she said, "I sense danger."

"What makes you say that?"

"I recall you saying the chimney and the stove grates are no good and Judith won't let Frank fix them because that's how they were when her father used the lodge. The four of them will be cooking and eating at Susan and Greg's. Familiarity doesn't breed contempt, it breeds desperation for privacy. If Mark and Teri don't get a house right away, Greg will be hiding upstairs every time they knock on the door."

"They are going to have their meals together. Mark asked Greg if it was okay and he said yes. I don't think it will be a problem. They all like each other a lot."

"What did you say about Teri? She'd be great for a motel week-end ... if you were deaf. She'll drive Susan and Greg crazy with her vacuous babbling. Believe me, darling, there'll be a problem."

Jessie had a piece of news for me.

Kept in the dark about the lake outing — Greg feared he'd turn up to scrounge a free meal — Frank had dropped by our house. Undoubtedly disgruntled that my wife wasn't feeling well enough to fix a proper lunch, he munched on soda crackers and an apple. Their conversation happened to light upon a dream Judith had five days prior to her last birthday. In the dream Jessie and I were piling our belongings in the box of the Black Bobcat. The house windows were boarded up; a "For Sale" sign was stapled to the building. The clarity of the sleep images caused Judith to trust she was receiving a privileged communiqué from an invisible power that had, or was about to, sway us into leaving the land. Assuring herself we'd be willing to unload the quarter section for next to nothing, she had invited us to the birthday celebration, expecting to slip an offer into the festive mix. Weeks later, when she was on her feet and talking to her son, Greg vigorously denied we were abandoning ship. Judith put her offer on hold. The Fergusons are trying hard, bless their souls, but, she firmly maintained, they're city people and some-day, sure as the sun shines and rivers flow, they'll realize they aren't cut out to be raggedy hillbillies.

25

Maya was running. She had parted company with Bella and was galloping towards the house. What had panicked her? A bear? A bobcat? I couldn't see anything in the yard. I glanced at Alex. He was stacking split poplars on the woodpile. His back was turned and he was unaware of the goat's sudden sprint. I hurried up the field. I called to Alex and he swung around as Maya was negotiating the porch steps. He was racing to apprehend her as she bunted the door open. The goat hadn't panicked; she was taking advantage of my son's neglect. He had forgotten to attach the hook and eye. By the time I made it to the house, Alex was pulling Maya's horns and Jessie was extracting the sleeve of a Mexican peasant blouse from the goat's mouth.

"You should've seen her when I came downstairs," Jessie said. "She was standing in the kitchen gaping at everything, and I could tell she loved the idea of being there. The forbidden zone. I'll swear she didn't intend to eat the blouse. She grabbed it to make me try to take it from her. It was her idea of fun."

On that day, a new game was devised.

Galloping Nanny.

If Maya was nearby and observing his actions, Alex connected the door latch roughly nine times out of ten, crushing her ambition. The tenth time he'd deliberately fail to secure the latch and casually walk to a spot a short distance away. He usually caught up with Maya on the porch, but she did burst into the kitchen more than once and stood frozen, savouring her victory, not knowing that Alex had, in a pre-game, cautionary manoeuvre, concealed the food, cookbooks, cutlery, and assorted objects that might appear delicious to a snatch-and-swallow diner. One afternoon, inventing a more complex version of Galloping Nanny, Alex sauntered around the far side of the building and then bolted to the front door. He sprang from the living room as Maya invaded the kitchen. He counted on startling and confusing her, but she looked at him without a flicker of surprise. Her hearing was so extraordinary that she likely detected the sound of his feet hitting the ground and the front door opening and shutting. Pushme-Pullme was another game. Alex grasped Maya's horns and attempted to drag her forward. She surrendered a little territory, held her ground, surrendered a little more. He switched objectives, trying to shove her backwards. Her strength was superior to his. He couldn't move her. When he released her horns, she stepped back, head lowered, and waited for the game to resume. Often, in an exceptionally playful mood, she reared up on her hind legs.

Alex and Maya were such happy playmates that I was sorry I had to take a chance on ruining their relationship. I was renting a buck (a.k.a. billy goat) for a week in anticipation of his impregnating Maya and Bella and bolstering our milk rations. Birthing babies had a grievous effect on some females; I hoped Maya wasn't one of those peppy, irresponsible, good-time girls motherhood transformed into responsible, over-protective, snarky-tempered whiners.

"Should I come with you?" my wife asked as I climbed into the Black Bobcat.

"No, it's all right. Stay and garden."

"I can help load the goat on the truck."

"It isn't necessary. The guy said he'd load him with planks. The buck will march straight up them."

The buck owner pastured his flock on both sides of the long driveway leading to his stuccoed duplex and in a hay field behind the house. Nearing the property, I took the animals to be white Saanens, but they weren't goats, they were sheep, every last one of them. Which was a novelty. In the three years I had been in northern Alberta, I hadn't seen a solitary sheep.

A heavy-set man in his fifties emerged from the barn. His sun-burnished face was cross-hatched with deep crevices.

"You must be the goat fellow that phoned me."

"Yes."

"How's the weather where you are?"

"Fine."

"The radio's calling for rain, but I don't see none."

"No, the sky's pretty clear."

"Did you get to Frontier Daze yesterday?"

"I'm afraid not."

"The wife came over fevery and I had to nurse her. No matter. Friday's *Gazette* will report the results. I was rooting for Dunc Belitski in the tire-rolling. It isn't fair him being second to Donny Swanson time and again. Donny practises for months, rolling tires up and down his hallway."

"I didn't know anybody in this area had sheep."

"The agriculture experts in Ottawa are forever nagging farmers to diversify. Scrap crops like barley, they say, which don't pay so hot anymore, and plant fava beans. There's nothing romantic about fava beans. No history worth repeating. Sheep, on the other hand, have a history. A hundred years ago cattlemen fought sheep farmers in this province over fencing and free-range grazing. There was violence. Shootings and blockading railway tracks. Somebody should write a book. Tell the country Canadians had their sheep wars, same as Americans."

"Yes, I suppose so."

"You'll be wanting to fetch the billy. He's in the barn."

The buck was standing in a stall: a large-headed, solid-bodied animal with curling horns and long, matted hair. He exuded an air of strutting, perpetually erect masculinity, and I was confident he'd have no difficulty adding Maya and Bella to his tally of conquests, providing they didn't mind the odour. He smelled like an alley drunk's shirt, the one he threw up on twice a week and washed twice a year.

The sheep farmer circled the buck's neck with a loose-hanging rope and walked him to the truck. The buck stood patiently as his owner placed planks between the dirt and the pickup box. I followed the path of the goat's alert gaze and saw he was mesmerized by a cluster of pastured sheep.

"Look at that bugger," the farmer said. "Can't keep his eyes off them. I locked him in the barn 'cause he was mounting the sheep and scaring them witless. I don't need no half and halfs. Half goat, half sheep. Spoils the burgers."

"The burgers?"

"People eat cows at McDonald's, so why not sheep at a lamb burger chain. Serve them with fries and onion rings. Name them something cute like Big Woolies. I've talked to the bank and the bank won't finance me so I'm going to Proctor and Gamble."

"The soap company?"

"The soap company. They must be primed to branch into a brand new business. They're mandated to spend their profits somewhere besides marbling the executive toilets."

As he forecast, the buck mounted the planks without a qualm. He tied the goat to the box, slackly to facilitate a possible impulse to lie down. Facing the cab, the goat twisted his neck to ogle the grass-chewing sheep. Great, I thought. He's lusting after the sheep so much he'll be leaping in the air and whooping when he's left alone with two members of his own species. By nightfall Maya and Bella will be knitting baby clothes or whatever it is pregnant goats do in advance of motherhood.

"The servicing fee — I have the cash on me."

"What servicing fee?"

"I was informed you charge for borrowing the buck."

"Informed by who?"

"The red-headed clerk at the feed store."

"He was mistaken. I sold my nannies and I've no purpose for him. So keep the raunchy bugger; he's yours, no charge."

Excellent.

We'd bathe the buck and trim his hair and have a permanent seed-dispenser in our possession. I drove off the farm and wheeled along a gravel road, striving to concoct an appropriate name for the buck, something reflecting his stud-muffin status. Johann Sebastian Bach fathered twenty children, but he was plump and homely and no one except his exhausted wives

back roads
Ted Ferguson

thought of him as a sexual powerhouse. The Marquis de Sade was too debauched, Georges Simenon too obnoxious for me to lay eyes on the goat every day and think of him. Sean Connery. Yes, he was the perfect role model for a buck. His towering form radiated studhorse manliness; at the sound of his voice in a darkened movie theatre a hundred ovaries cried, "Use me!"

A short distance from the highway, Sean Connery commenced banging his head against the cab. Hard bangs, enraged bangs, bangs proclaiming that if he didn't escape the truck post-haste he'd smash past the metal and bunt me through the windshield. It had to be the motion that was upsetting him. The jarring and swaying, the blurry rush of the unfamiliar countryside. I slowed to a crawl and turned onto the deserted highway pointing towards the Dunes. He stopped banging. I crept a few miles up the road and then he went at it again: blasting, pausing, blasting. Pivoting my head, I saw blood trickling from a forehead gash. I braked and jumped onto asphalt. The buck froze, his eyes on the cab, shunning me.

How far was it to the homestead? Twenty miles, bare minimum.

How long would it take to walk there?

Leading a goat on a rope, climbing the hill ascending to the Dunes, perspiring, resting, cursing, dreading he'd spy a deer he'd be compelled to race after and mount: three hours, bare minimum.

The wound wasn't deep. If I drove faster, I'd be home in twenty minutes and Jessie could patch him up.

I stalled, uncertain which option to seize.

The buck resolved the dilemma. He thawed himself, ramming the cab again. He was in such an up-your-rump mood that walking him to the Dunes would be a nightmare, Pushme-Pullme minus the game aspect. I slid into the truck and pushed the accelerator down. The buck reactivated his blast-pause-blast pattern. Somewhere on the other side of the hill, he ceased bunting. I glanced over my shoulder. He had surrendered to his destiny; he was reclining. I turned off the highway and drove to my property. When I alighted at the gate, he didn't lift his head to see what was going on. In fact, he wasn't stirring at all; he had rammed the cab so hard he knocked himself unconscious. I swung the gate open, clambered onto the box, and inspected the goat. He wasn't unconscious. His eyes were cold and motionless and he wasn't breathing. Sean Connery was dead.

Why?

What had happened to him?

Did he crush his brain assaulting the truck? Did he suffer a fatal heart attack? Was he depressed about leaving his beloved home and so committed suicide? The cause of the buck's death wasn't my chief concern, disposing of the carcass was. The municipality banned the tossing of animal remains in the local dump. I hadn't the strength to pick him up and cart him into the woods — he weighed well over a hundred pounds — and I hadn't the stomach for hacking him into smaller portions to fit the barrel we burned our trash in.

As I deliberated, a vehicle sped my way. A yellow truck, hurling dust. The truck halted behind the Black Bobcat. It belonged to the telephone company. The hard-hatted driver said he had forgotten to bring his copy of the Dunes' map identifying area landowners and, relying on his memory of a cursory map examination, he scoured the wrong routes for an hour.

"I'm here to say we're laying cable next week," he said. "We'll go down the centre of your property road? Underground, naturally. You won't be able to tell the cable's there." He glanced at the buck without a glimmer of curiosity, as if a dead goat tied to a truck was a daily sight. "How far in's your house?"

"Half a mile."

"Don't worry, sir. You'll soon be able to phone an ambulance."

An ambulance?

"I suppose you never know when you'll need one."

"Especially in your case."

In my case?

The telephone man rolled up his window and departed.

Jessie was in the garden, gathering lettuce and tomatoes for a dinner salad.

back
roads
Ted
Ferguson

"Where's the Bobcat?"

"Above the hill."

"With the buck in it?"

"He stinks like hell. To me, anyway. Maybe the smell's an aphrodisiac to Maya and Bella. I was afraid of them going crazy and throwing themselves at a dead goat."

"Did I hear that correctly? You went to somebody's farm and rented a dead goat?"

I leaned on the garden fence and recounted my experience.

"There's a pet cemetery in Edmonton," I said, "but I doubt they'll accept a goat. Their specialty is overwrought poodles and overweight cats."

"Leave him on Crown land."

"That's an idea."

"Who goes on Crown land? Only hunters."

I devised a simple-minded system to unload the goat. Determining the rope securing the dead animal to the box was too short for my purpose, I retrieved a longer piece and walked up the hill. A skunk was hurrying into the bush — it couldn't bear the buck's smell.

Locating a disposal site for the goat wasn't easy. Thickly wooded, most of the Crown land extended to the lip of the road, and somehow it seemed disrespectful to the buck to force him to rot in full public view. I cruised the Dunes, passing uninhabited woods the regional map specified as Crown property. Finally, I found a satisfactory dumping ground: a clearing beside the road. I drove to the rear of the clearing, undid the box rope, attached one end of the long rope to the goat's hind legs and the other end to the base of a sturdy tree. When I accelerated, the goat slid off the truck onto his eternal resting place.

In the fading light of the fading summer, my wife went to the Polish Widow's store. The door was bolted. She walked around to the garden. The elderly woman was on her knees, talking to a cabbage. Breaking off the whispered monologue, she straightened her willowy body, squeezed Jessie's arm and said, "You good mother. I show you secret."

She took Jessie across the empty highway, through a shoulder-high thicket and into a shaded gully.

"Look see," she said. "Best mushrooms grow. You pick them. Not now. Now they are mine. You pick when I am old and can't cross road."

The Polish Widow asked about our mulching experiment, the potatoes I buried beneath a pile of decaying hay. Jessie had a little tale for her. A farmer who consented to plant oats showed up unexpectedly to inspect our field while we were in town. He saw the disintegrating hay and, believing he was doing us a favour, he lifted it with his tractor's front-end loader and deposited it part-way down the field, somewhere in the bush. Agreeing the experiment was destroyed, we didn't bother searching for the pile. On a walk, months afterwards, I chanced upon it. Brushing hay aside, I was amazed to discover a crop of healthy potatoes.

The Polish Widow had a little tale for my wife.

Two young men working for an oil company seismic crew had come to her store. They were charting exploratory readings on a quarter section northwest of her property.

"Lunatics everywhere!" the Polish Widow exclaimed. "I lock window, sleep with scissors!"

The two young men, she said, had found something revoltingly evil. They had found a dead goat with its back legs roped to a tree.

26 By the existing concepts of the international art trade, Greg's latest carving constituted a deplorable misunderstanding between his head and his hand. The figures lacked detailed refinement, the cowboy in the saddle was disproportionately large for the horse. I may not have admired the sculpture, but I was impressed by Greg's ability to mould a single block of wood into an object his wife reverently displayed on their coffee table.

"Isn't he a genius?" Susan asked, pouring herbal tea into our cups.

"A single block of wood," I said. "I'm impressed."

Greg appeared to be vastly delighted with himself, but, emulating the fake modesty that major artists conjure to disguise the self-adoring egotism Canadians despise, he said disparagingly, "The saddle horn's too close to the rider. It looks like he's got a hard-on."

"No, it doesn't," Susan laughed.

"Sure it does. Know what I'm titling it? 'Cowboy Heading to Whorehouse.'"

"That'll go over big at the exhibit," Susan said.

"What exhibit?" Jessie asked.

"The Edmonton Art Gallery. Greg's doing a slew of cowboy sculptures: branding cattle, roping calves, et cetera. I'll be his agent and show it to the curator. He's bound to dig it. Cowboy art's a hot commodity. Greg will be rich and famous."

"The Edmonton Art Gallery's a government institution," Jessie said. "It doesn't sell the works it exhibits."

"You must be wrong," Susan said adamantly. "They must sell it. Even government bureaucrats aren't stupid enough to support an art gallery that doesn't try to earn a profit."

Jessie sipped her tea and said nothing.

I copied her. I offered no argument to Susan's statement, but I did give it some thought. Susan and Greg had leapt off the nine-to-five treadmill and claimed not to care about society beyond the

Dunes. But they weren't Buddhist monks, they weren't praying and meditating to eradicate personal desire. Susan and Greg had their dreams, their fantasies, like the rest of us deluded earthlings, and a priority dream, a priority fantasy, concerned people outside the Dunes recognizing that Greg was a gifted person tailored from exquisite cloth. If Susan chose to think the Edmonton Art Gallery sold wood carvings, if she chose to think Greg's work warranted fame and monetary success, then let her revel in the illusion until the gallery curator spoke the stinging truth.

"My dad was here yesterday," Greg said. "Now I know something you don't know."

"Impossible," I said. "I know everything."

"He told me how he scored the phone for you."

"Really? He won't tell me."

"He was worried you'd be mad."

"Why would I be mad?"

"He went to the AGT office and said your son was a hemophiliac. He cuts himself, he bleeds to death, unless you phone for an ambulance."

"I don't believe it."

"You're mad."

"No, I'm not mad. I just can't believe he'd go to all that trouble for a sack of carrots."

Actually, it wasn't that difficult to believe. Most people discarded junk in the municipal dump — Frank descended the trash-littered slopes of the smouldering, stinking hollow to drag junk out. The Arborite table in his kitchen was a dump gleaning. He fixed the broken leg and, as Judith was apt to be mortified by its origin, he told her he traded hay for it. The steel barrel in his truck box, filled with bargain-rate purple gas, was from the dump as was the black and white TV set he sold at the Sunnyside auction.

"Frank isn't a Judith," Susan said. "She's a cheapskate because she's obsessed with money. Scoring free stuff's a hobby for him. He does it to entertain himself when he isn't glued to his wife's apron strings."

back
roads
Ted
Ferguson

"He's Susan's competition," Greg said.

"Last week I asked a guy renovating a shop for his old rug," Susan said. "Frank had asked him that morning and was coming for it later. Isn't that a gas? Two scroungers competing for a rug and they're both from the same family."

"I hear a car," Greg said, whipping to his feet.

I didn't hear anything, but that didn't mean a car wasn't in his yard. Greg's faculty for detecting faint sounds rivalled our goats'.

"Mark and Teri," he said from the window. "The pot's empty. Put the kettle on again."

"The gods aren't smiling on us," Mark said, flopping onto a chair.

"I'm doing tea," Susan said. "Mint."

"Super," Teri said.

"We didn't see a single house we'd be happy living in," Mark said.

"Don't say we," Teri teased. "Mister Picky turned his nose up at all of them but his wife didn't. He's worse than an old lady."

"I'm not picky," Mark said defensively. "I simply want a place with a distinct personality."

"Such as?" Greg asked.

"I don't know. High ceilings, bay windows, a banister staircase. Georgian, Victorian, or a house in harmony with nature. In the style of Frank Lloyd Wright. Most of the real estate on the market between here and the other side of Preston is in the style of Lawrence Welk."

"Lawrence Welk?" Susan smiled. "Since when did he design houses?"

"He didn't, but if he did they'd cater to common taste. Nouveau Mundane. The cookie-cutter school of architecture best exemplified in modern suburbia. Houses that aren't in harmony with nature. Houses that are in harmony with every other building on the block."

"Oh, I get it," Greg said. "You're looking for a house with an oak tree in the bedroom and a duck pond in the den."

"It doesn't have to be an oak tree," Mark said humorously. "I'll settle for spruce."

The exchange between the four friends swept Jessie and I into the shadows. We were visible, we could be heard, but our light diminished in comparison to Mark and Teri's brilliant wattage. This wasn't the first time I was conscious of Greg and Susan responding so ardently to the other couple that I felt as if my wife and I had been demoted for not measuring up to Mark's preeminent charm and Teri's facial glory.

"It took us a while to find our place," I said.

"Yes, Greg told me," Mark said. "But you were short of cash and looking for a deal. The price isn't that essential to me."

"You're in no rush," Greg said. "My mother won't be evicting you from the lodge. The way she talks about you, you've got at least ten years to find a place."

"We did see a big, old house that bowled Mark over," Teri said. "He changed his tune inside."

"God, that was bizarre," Mark said, shaking his head.

"Was it ever," Teri said. "I was gaping like a retard."

"The living room floor was covered with white tiles," Mark said. "There were tiles halfway up the walls. It was like walking into a public toilet. I asked the owner's wife why it was done that way and she said, 'My husband's with a construction company in Edmonton. He comes home weekends and he brings leftover tiles.' I guess if he was employed at a condom factory he'd do the room with the rejects."

"I'd kill to have a tiled living room," Greg said. "It's easier to clean. Turn on the tap and hose it down."

"You're hilarious," Teri said.

The kettle rattled. Susan poured the water into the pot.

"When we were going to the Toilet Palace we passed a field with goats in it," Mark said. "We saw some baby goats, so there has to be a billy somewhere. Maybe the farmer will lend him to you guys."

"We won't be needing him," I said.

"Aren't you breeding your goats?"

"No, we've decided against starting a goat farm. Too much hassle."

back roads
Ted Ferguson

{165}

I didn't elaborate.

I didn't feel it was necessary to divulge that we decided against starting the farm because our knowledge of goat behaviour and maintenance was ludicrously superficial. Sean Connery had opened our eyes to that. We had discussed his death and the entire scheme to breed and market goats and we found ourselves speculating upon the possible consequences if the buck hadn't died. What if he was a savage-tempered renegade, prone to biting and bunting? What if he was sterile or impotent or a fanatical misogynist? What if, in my ignorance of medical warning signs, I had accepted a goat with a contagious disease or rotting hooves or a fragile heart nearing its expiry date? What if his hideous smell was permanent, a genetic ailment peculiar to male adult goats, alley-drunk-odourisis? And what if he had survived the journey and fathered a batch of kids? We were, to state it plainly, ill-equipped to provide first-class care should any or all of them suffer drastic health problems.

It was, as I told Mark, too much hassle.

We were, after all, supposed to be simplifying our lives, reducing the chances of future stress and strain. Less is more, Mies van der Rohe said, and although the wealthy architect was probably dwelling amid a mammoth array of materialistic clutter when he said it, he did have a point worth adopting as a guidepost. In the final summation, the goat farm was a naive and romanticized balloon that popped the day Sean Connery dropped dead.

"Are you keeping the goats you already have?" Mark asked.

"Definitely," I said. "They're family pets."

"Teri has her heart set on owning a horse."

"A black mare with a white patch on its nose shaped like a diamond," Teri said. "I saw one in a movie."

"Which reminds me," Mark said. "*A Day at the Races* is playing at the Dreamland."

"Along with *A Night to Remember*," Greg said.

"You've seen the ad in the *Gazette*."

"Nope. Evanko always runs those films together."

"The thing is, Teri and I are driving in tonight. Do you want to go with us?"

"Not me. How about you, Susan? You're a Marx Brothers fan."

Susan made no reply.

I transferred my eyes to where she had stationed herself, against the counter, next to the stove. She was staring at the floor, arms folded, with the morose focus of a graveside mourner.

"Hey, Susan, wakey-wakey," Mark said. "Elvis Presley's here. He's begging for you to comb his sideburns."

Susan's head jolted up. She looked at Mark as though he had said something unforgivably infuriating.

"The tea should be ready," Greg said.

"Get it yourself," Susan snapped, walking to the door trailing rage.

Teri fixed the tea.

When Jessie and I left for home, Susan was sitting on a stump near the barn. She ignored us.

"Trouble in paradise," Jessie said.

There was trouble, all right, but I was unable to identify its source. Nor could I estimate its depth. So far, I had spotted hairline fractures: the cemetery stare, her refusal to serve the tea, and the anti-Greg slashing at the swimming hole. Nothing that didn't occur in most marriages, but Susan's attitude towards Greg was unlike that of most wives. Her worshipful love, I had assumed, was total and irrevocable, casting a luminous glow and eliminating the dimmest chance of marital conflict.

back
roads
Ted
Ferguson

27

Winter came late and, making up for its tardiness, filled the November landscape with thick ice and drifting snow and sharp winds ambitious to cut the flesh from your bones. Icicles clutched eaves, frost drew gorgeous, senseless patterns on window glass. Radio reporters recited terms like "deep freeze" and "no end in sight" and warned seniors against treading on icy sidewalks in case they fell and broke their hips. *The Noonday Knee-Slapper* relayed jokes about earmuffs and long johns, frozen udders, temperamental wives with cabin fever, and moronic boys freezing their tongues to railway tracks.

With the municipal road snowed under we were temporarily severed from the main body of contemporary civilization. We didn't feel deprived. We were a chatty threesome, good-spirited and comfortable in each other's company, and as weather-forced confinement can yield discord and a floor-pacing craving to escape the trap, we deemed ourselves fortunate. When the winds calmed, when the sky coloured itself a sublime blue, we revelled in the sweet silence, the sense that it was ours and ours alone — the valley, the northland, the sprawling, unmanageable, beguilingly beautiful universe.

Mornings commenced with the dogs flying outside and one of us freeing the goats, a chore that sometimes involved shovelling a path to their shed. Maya was intolerant of delays. The second she heard the dogs hit the yard she began bunting the shed door. Blowing snow or a scathing wind persuaded her to run up the path to the steps, check to see whether or not the passageway to the forbidden zone was barred, and then race back to the shed, where she and Bella stood in the doorway, eyes sweeping the yard, like sentries looking for saboteurs. Attempts to shut the door and shield them from the weather met with Maya's frenzied bunting. After breakfast, Jessie collected firewood from the yard pile to top up the porch woodbox, and Alex dragged plastic containers up from the well on the sled. I lugged the coal bucket to the house and the Winnipeg heater. I had acted upon Brother Henri's advice and built a coal bin, using the technique I revived later for the garage, nailing boards between four sawed-off poplars. Alas, I was unqualified to conduct a skilled judgment and the boards I selected at the lumberyard were cut from green timber. They dried, shrank, and warped, exposing the coal to sunlight and creating a rollicking knee-slapper for the dark-robed ruler of The Servants of the Adored Blood.

Changing the root cellar lamp was my chore. I left a low-burning kerosene lamp on a shelf above the vegetable sacks whenever the temperature fell below zero. Four days after a series of blizzards closed the road, I mounted the root cellar ladder, stepped outside, and heard the snowplow. I carried the empty lamp to the house. My wife was feeding the dogs. Drake had missed Joe for a month or so. He had barely eaten his meals and had lain at the foot of the hill, presumably waiting for Joe's camper to sail over the summit. He had gradually adapted to the change and become attached to us. Some nights he'd jump on the bed and sleep at our feet. Rocky still growled if anyone tried to touch him, but, speaking gently and moving slowly, Jessie coaxed him to a stage where he no longer bared his teeth when she laid a food bowl in front of him.

"The plow's clearing the road," I said begrudgingly. "I'll go to the city tomorrow. I've lost my excuse for staying home."

"Take the Honda," Jessie said, turning from the dogs. "Then I won't have to pick you up in Preston."

"I can't leave you here without the car. What if there's an emergency? The snow's too deep to drive the truck to the gate."

"We have a phone now. I can call for help." She smiled and added, "I'll scratch Alex's finger and phone for an ambulance."

The next morning, I donned my going-to-the-city duffel coat and transported a suitcase and car battery on the sled to the garage. I warmed the Honda block with the propane torch and shovelled a snowdrift away from the garage entrance. In the car, the heater humming, I wriggled into my professional writer costume, replacing soiled jeans with wool trousers, a bulky, cable-knit sweater with an Oleg Cassini pullover, and the clunky snow boots with black Italian loafers. I had arranged to interview the octogenarian oil company chairman who cultivated orchids and collected vintage automobiles. During the Depression, he had operated a rural medical practice, furnishing his services to cash-parched farmers in exchange for the ownership of potential petroleum deposits on their land. The oil boom following the 1947 Leduc strike harvested a fortune for him. As the magazine I was writing the article for planned to include the ex-doctor in an issue saluting visionary business czars, I pre-determined that the word "swindler" would not appear in the story.

I spent three days in Edmonton interviewing the wealthy oilman and researching his company's successes and defeats. It snowed heavily the final day. Checking out of my motel, I phoned Jessie. I promised to return to the city and stay overnight at a motel if the highway linking Edmonton and Preston was bad. If the highway was okay but the less diligently maintained Dunes highway looked terrible, I would hole up at the Preston Hotel.

I missed my family. I missed the dogs. I missed the goats.

After three nights in an overheated hotel room, watching television and eating take-out food, I felt stranded and lonely. Despite my promise to my wife, I drove north on the icy, snow-blown highway, passing two cars mangled in a head-on confrontation and creeping through a white-out. By the time I reached the Preston turn-off, the sun was gone. Breaking my second promise, I took the Dunes route.

I drove slowly, white-knuckling the steering wheel and peering rigidly into the headlight beams, dreading black ice, darting animals, and a semi roaring out of the blizzard.

I made it to the municipal road.

It was buried in snow.

No problem. The Honda had front-wheel traction.

I veered onto the road and accelerated. The Honda shot forward, penetrating the snow without faltering. I went up and down small hills and skirted a tree that had partly fallen across the road. All of a sudden, the car engine went dead. Because the lights and heater died with it, I figured the battery cables had shaken loose. I put on my snow boots, grabbed the glove compartment flashlight, popped the hood, and hopped out. The space between the radiator and the block was packed solid with snow. I inspected the battery and the engine. The cables were secure and the motor heat melted the snow rising up the sides, but the sparkplugs, alternator, and generator cap were wet. I went to the hatch to retrieve the shovel. It wasn't there. I had forgotten to return it to its customary spot after I cleared the garage drift. I grabbed the jack handle. In lieu of digging, I punched holes in the snow. When I had freed the radiator fan and assured myself that the hose was firmly attached, I tried starting the engine. It didn't respond. I decided to walk the rest of the way home. It was only two miles — no big deal for a habitual hiker.

Trudging up the road, clasping the flashlight, I formed a Honda recovery plan. The hour the plow reopened the municipal road, I'd trek to the car and wipe the engine parts dry. Furthermore, on my trip to Preston I'd buy a shovel exclusively for the Honda — and never again drive in snow in a vehicle with a motor close to the ground.

The wind was wickedly aggressive, a classic Prairie soul-chiller, and the snow bore down the middle of the road, hitting me straight-on, and restricted the flashlight illumination. And that wasn't the worst part of it. The worst was the snow already on the road. Some of the drifts were over two feet deep. The legs that conveyed me through summer woods without a whisper of unfaithfulness suddenly turned disloyal. They seemed weighty and depleted, resistant to each new step. I grew alarmed, remembering a newspaper story about an injured farmer freezing to death two hundred yards from his home. And I remembered Robert Redford. In *Jeremiah Johnson* he stumbled upon a frozen corpse sitting upright in the wilderness. I couldn't allow that to happen to me. I feared death as much as any mortal did, but more than my own death, I was horrified by the prospect of devastating my family, of causing an unmendable tear in their lives.

I pictured the house: shining lights, smoking chimney. I struggled forward, holding that image as if it were a holy vision. Sweat wettened my skin, a queer state of affairs considering the sub-zero air, and I longed to stand still for more than a few seconds and, an even stronger urge, to go into the brush and rest against the base of a tree.

Finally, the gate loomed.

I went through it oddly relieved, as though nothing was liable to harm me now that I was on my own land.

A dark, lumpish form caught my eye at the foot of the tarpaulin covering the garage entrance. I swung the light. Three or four dogs were huddled together. A head jolted up. I lowered the beam and moved faster. Wild dogs had a reputation for brutality.

The snow wasn't as deep on my tree-sheltered road, but it was still hard slogging.

I looked over my shoulder. A large, black, hairless mongrel was standing on the road, snarling. I kept walking, propelling my legs, glancing behind. The mongrel was following me. It halted every time the beam struck it. Other dark shapes materialized. Three dogs, trailing the mongrel.

Wild dog packs existed on their kills but, I reminded myself, they were not known to fancy human food. Then why were they pursuing me? Not for friendly purposes, that was for sure. The pack leader seemed to be waiting for me to collapse. It had the demeanor of an animal wishing to rip a hole in somebody's throat, just for a flash of excitement.

At the crest of the hill I swept the beam behind me and witnessed the mongrel going into the bush. The other dogs followed it. What compelled the mongrel to end the pursuit? Did it spy a rabbit or something else it wanted to kill? Or was it rewarding my determination, like a matador permitting a courageous bull to survive? The reason really didn't matter. The dog had vanished and my throat was safe.

I plunged down the hill.

The house lay in darkness. Jessie and Alex were sleeping. I climbed the steps and banged on the bolted door. The dogs barked, and then I heard my wife's voice. The door swung open, and then the house encircled me, warm and intimate, in the embrace of a comforting lover.

Frank's pickup cruised into view as I was ratcheting a sparkplug out of the Honda. He idled his truck and alighted, visibly wary. He had grown tired of fixing the Black Bobcat whenever he dropped by for a meal and it was misbehaving. Doctors loathed receiving medical inquiries outside office hours; Frank loathed working on other people's vehicles. I empathized with him — I loathed having people ask me to write stories for nothing — but, nevertheless, I felt justified prodding him into doing minor repairs. His labour was the bill for all those scrounged dinners and lunches.

"The Honda giving you grief?" he asked disagreeably, as if the car was a bawling baby with a poop-crammed diaper he didn't want to change.

"It won't start. I think the plugs are wet. I was driving here before the MD ploughed the road. Snow rose up from underneath and covered them."

"The plugs splutter?"

"No, everything suddenly conked out."

"Lousy Jap cars. What you save on gas, you spend in the shop. Small stuff. Nickel-and-diming you to the poorhouse." He sighed and drew his gloved hands from his coat pockets. "Shove over, I'll take a shot at it." He fiddled with the generator and the alternator, attached a disconnected wire I'd missed seeing and used his cables to boost the cold battery. "Try her now," he said.

I twisted the ignition key. The motor resurrected.

"You're in business again," Frank said.

"Terrific. Thank you."

"How'd you get home after the car broke down?"

"On foot."

"Jeez. It's colder than a prostitute's you-know-what. Lucky you weren't frost-bitten. I'll tail you. I've something to tell you folks."

"What is it?"

"I'll say it at the house. Then I won't be repeating myself for your wife."

I parked the Honda in the garage, extracted the battery, and laid it on the sled. The snow that had fallen around the garage since I'd encountered the wild dogs was free of animal tracks. As I hadn't seen any on the road walking up from the house, I gathered the mongrel and its friends had kept on travelling.

We hiked to the house, Frank trudging close behind the sled.

"Judith's fit to be tied," he said.

"How come?"

"She's a moral person. She can't abide decadence."

"Whose decadence can't Judith abide?"

"I'll explain in a minute. We're almost there."

Jessie was busy. She dumped ashes, fed the goats, and rounded up root-cellar vegetables. Frank waited for her to complete the chores. While I fixed coffee, he flipped through a magazine and, flying in the face of his proclaimed aversion to repeating himself, he described, for the third time that month, a National Film Board short he'd seen at a community centre movie night. In the film, a salesman arrives in a winter-bound Prairie town to find the streets deserted and the stores shut. Where was everyone? Had they all gone home early? Were they all victims of a mysterious epidemic? The salesman searched and searched and ultimately discovered the entire town, every man, woman and child, was at the curling rink. The film irritated Frank. The ignorant Easterners who made it were telling the world that Prairie-dwellers were a bunch of yokels with nothing better to do than play with brooms and rocks. Plenty of things on the Prairies deserved a movie more than curling did. The history of grain elevators, for instance. And the people devoting their blood, sweat, and tears to small-town life. People like the Frontier Daze volunteers and the pioneering entrepreneur who opened the first fast-food outlet in Preston: the A&W next to the Mohawk station.

Jessie came in, and poured herself a coffee.

"So how are you doing, Frank?"

"Not too good. Mark's taken off."

"Taken off? What do you mean?"

"He's in Vancouver and he isn't coming back. I don't blame him, knowing the circumstances."

"What circumstances?" I asked.

Sometime last August, Frank had gone to Greg and Susan's to give his son a windbreaker he'd gotten for a buck at the Goodwill. The Mustang and Mark's car were both absent from the yard and, unless he was hiding in a closet, Greg wasn't home. Frank had a library book Judith thought Mark would be keen on reading, *The Canadian Establishment*. He decided to leave it at the lodge. Mark and Teri were probably house-hunting, and he could investigate Susan's housekeeping to be certain she wasn't slacking off. On the path, Greg and Teri sauntered towards him, facing each other and looking pleased as punch. Greg's arm hugged Teri's shoulders. When they set eyes on him, Greg didn't drop his arm and neither of them looked guilty. Maybe they were really affectionate pals and that's all there was to it, but Frank couldn't shake the notion that he had chanced upon an awful truth: Greg and Teri shared an intimacy the Lord intended married people to only share with their legal spouses. Now he knew his suspicion was bang-on. Last week he stopped by Greg and Susan's and sensed straight off that something was different; the ground had shifted. Teri was there and the three of them were speaking in a kind of code, tiny asides and jokes that winged over his head. Asking where Mark was prompted Susan to answer that he and Teri split up and Mark was in Vancouver. Teri and Susan laughed when Greg said Mark loved spinning tales, so they'd invented a juicy one for him to spin. Frank put up with their asides and in-jokes awhile, drinking rosehip tea and talking about nothing in particular. As he was departing, Greg peered right in his face and said, as though his chief goal that day was to upset him, "You might as well know this: Teri's living with us. We don't have piece of paper to prove it but she's my wife the same as Susan is."

Frank took it in his stride — or so he said — but Judith was thrown for a loop.

"Greg wasn't considering his mother's sensitivity when he got Teri to shack up," Frank lamented. "Judith's hurting. She's afraid of the humiliation, Wally Gossip circulating the story. Folks tend to blame the mother for not raising her child properly."

"I wouldn't worry," Jessie said. "Greg and Susan don't have any friends in Preston. They won't be telling anybody."

"Yeah, well, that don't count for a whole lot. People see and hear things and put two and two together. Sooner or later, everyone will know. I said to Judith that she ought to boot them out of the house. Then maybe they'd bugger off to the city. She won't go for it. Greg's her son. She's suffering but she'll learn to cope with the situation."

So would Jessie and I.

We weren't suffering as severely as Judith was, but we were hurt that Susan hadn't trusted us enough to be more forthcoming. Instead, she sent weak signals that only seemed clear now that we knew the score: her apprehension over Mark and Teri's pending visit (Greg must have had a past affair with Teri, or he'd expressed his desire to seduce her), the swimming pool complaints (evidently designed to turn Teri off Greg), and the day she blew up and stormed outside (more than likely, she had just discovered Greg was sleeping with Teri). At one time in my life, I would've pictured Greg in bed with the two females and been stricken by an envy seizure. Now I was older and I understood it was not a paradisiacal situation. Sex was a small part of a ménage à trois; the complexities of daily existence, the minor grievances, and the simmering jealousies rubbed such relationships thin. I had seen *Jules and Jim*. I didn't expect Susan or Teri to drive off a pier but, stuck in a house together all winter, I did expect one of the women to break ranks long before the earth thawed.

Soon after sunset every night, Drake proceeded to the porch door and waited patiently to be let out. We had our regular chores, he had his. For anywhere between five and forty-five minutes, the duration governed by the weather, he lodged himself on the landing and discharged a fitful series of barks, mostly urgent and loud but occasionally feeble and diffident, more yelps than barks. The family consensus was that Drake was warning the unseen entities prowling the black woods — the coyotes, the bears, the bobcats, the serial killers, ghosts, and demons — that they wouldn't be welcome in our yard.

One frigid evening Drake fell silent within minutes of going outside. When the silence expanded, Jessie put down the novel she was reading and went to see if he was ready for the next phase of the ritual, scurrying inside to stretch on the floor inches from the kitchen stove. He wasn't on the landing. Jessie called his name, and when he failed to materialize she bundled herself in winter gear, got a flashlight, and walked into the cold. She scoured the yard and the top of the field and then mounted the hill. I was in Toronto, meeting editors, and she figured the dog may have thought he heard me returning, gone up the road, and anchored himself somewhere, risking hypothermia.

She found him on the road, lying in blood-stained snow, his stomach and his penis horribly chewed. Jessie ran to the house. She grabbed a down jacket to warm Drake's shivering body. Alex dressed hastily and took the battery to the sled. Jessie wrapped the dog in the jacket and carried him to the car. He didn't whimper, and he didn't struggle. He lay in her arms as if he were so shocked by what had occurred to him that his mind was as frozen as the dark terrain.

The veterinarian resided in a two-storey house on the outskirts of Preston. He was peddling an exercise bike in his living room. He pulled a parka over his sweatsuit and, untied boot

back
roads
Ted
Ferguson

laces flipping, accompanied my wife to the car. The clinic was next door to his house. The veterinarian placed Drake on an examination table. He gave him a shot and patched his wounds. The injury to the dog's abdomen would heal, but he confessed he hadn't the talent to repair the penis. Did anyone? Yes, his friend in Edmonton, a veterinary surgeon with the hands of a Christian Bernard. At Jessie's urging, he phoned his friend and asked him to open his clinic.

Jessie rushed through darkness to the city, Drake stretched on the rear seat, his head in Alex's lap. The veterinary surgeon met them at the door. He examined Drake, concluded the penis had to be amputated and that Drake needed to recover in a clinic kennel. Several days afterwards, the veterinary surgeon phoned to announce that the dog had gone under the knife: Drake, the Labrador male, was now Drake, the Labrador female. It was, the veterinary surgeon said, the first sex-change operation he performed on a dog.

Both the Edmonton and Preston veterinarians theorized that upon meeting his attacker Drake adopted a submissive gesture common to dogs, rolling onto his back. Both men believed the attacker was a member of a coyote pack. Jessie had no reason to disagree but she did wonder, and never ceased wondering, if Drake's assailant was actually the mongrel that followed me through the blizzard.

The avocado-green toaster was a conspicuous addition. So were the peach-coloured clock radio, the ceramic ashtray, and, sharing the coffee table with the cowboy sculpture, the Harlequin lamp with a pinkish shade. What else did Teri have shipped to her new home the very week she and Mark separated? Was there an Afghan bedspread upstairs? An off-white dresser and matching curtains? Packages of avocado-green condoms?

29

"It's been forever since we've seen you guys," Susan said. "What have you been up to?"

"Not a great deal," I replied. "Hanging around the house. Too cold to go anywhere."

Too cold, and too soon to visit them following Frank's surprising revelation that Greg had, physically if not lawfully, two wives. Greg would've known enlightening his father was the same as enlightening us. We had stayed away to avoid the impression that we were racing over to gawk, as though their unorthodox arrangement was a branch of entertainment devised to titillate the sexually less adventurous. Jessie also thought it best to skirt them until they were more amenable to having guests. "Let's give it a little time for the lust to settle," was how she expressed it.

"Frank told us about Drake," Susan said. "How does he like being a girl?"

"He hasn't said. Sometimes he lies on the floor staring at his crotch as if he's wondering why his penis fell into a sinkhole."

"He thinks he's a male," Jessie said. "He still lifts his leg to pee."

"I don't know whether or not the operation affected his sexual preference," I said. "We'll find out next summer when the Jehovah's Witness lady shows up. Will he or won't he hump her leg?"

Susan smiled, rather wanly, and twisted in her chair to address Teri. "Did Greg say where he was going?"

"The lodge."

"That was an hour ago."

"He's probably shovelling snow off the roof."

"Yeah, probably."

Teri was ensconced in the armchair, devoting herself to a craft familiar to generations of weather-trapped farm wives — knitting.

The sweater was lime green, Susan's favourite colour. Teri was strangely subdued. She knit one, purled one, and when Susan uncapped the wine we brought, a chokecherry product made from berries culled on our property, she declined a glass. Why wasn't she drinking? Was she scared of the cliché — the hackneyed supposition that alcohol loosened the tongue?

Susan, on the other hand, treated the wine like an essential tool for human preservation. She drained a glass and tore into a second, and although she kept her portion of the dialogue afloat, she appeared remote and disinterested. Had we come at a bad time? Did Susan and Teri just have a fight? Or was the tight, three-way relationship splitting at the seams and any time was a bad time?

"We saw an oil company truck on your road," Jessie said. "Are they drilling somewhere?"

"No," Susan said. "Cutting a trail to a well site. I told them they ought to be ashamed of themselves, killing trees without apologizing."

"Apologizing to who?" Jessie asked.

"The trees."

"The trees?"

"Aboriginals contend trees have spirits. They don't dare chop one down without saying they're sorry. Greg's been reading about Aboriginals lately. We want to be more like them. Reverence for the land, and the forest spirits."

"Indians have so much to teach us," Teri said.

"Greg's doing a series of Aboriginal carvings," Susan said. "Buffalo, canoes, and teepees."

"These sleeves don't look right," Teri said. "Can I try them again?"

Susan crossed the floor. Teri held the sweater against her body and declared the sleeves the ideal length. She said something in a low, secretive voice; the two women laughed hysterically. Susan clutched Teri's arm as though the remark weakened her ankles.

"What's so funny?" I asked.

"Nothing," Susan said. "A private joke."

It was then that the light blazed. It was then that I understood, or believed I understood, how the landscape was changing. Susan was not only excluding me from the joke, she was aiming to transfer the Fergusons to the foggy borders of her life. By some incredible and mysterious process, she had dissolved her negative feelings about Teri and attained a depth of closeness that, given Teri's affliction, a case of inoperable tedium, I never thought possible. And as Susan wouldn't act without Greg's approval, possessing two lovers must have produced a sense of completion, of wholeness, ridding him of any further need for friends. We were, at best, bothersome intruders in the seraglio. Perhaps I was reading too much into the proceedings — Susan's remoteness, the private joke, the familiarity implied by the grip on Teri's arm — but I left the house swearing that Greg hadn't gone to the lodge, he had darted upstairs the moment he knew whose car had driven past the gate.

Our friendship with Greg and Susan didn't end that afternoon. It staggered and stumbled, perishing in stages.

Knowing that I may have misinterpreted the situation, I took some magazines we were finished with to their house. The Tysons were always glad to receive a stack of reading material. Susan came to the door. Greg was ill and to spare myself a virus invasion I'd be wise not step inside.

"Is everything all right?" I asked sotto voce, seeking a whispered explanation to dispel my perception that the friendship was on death row. "Besides Greg being ill."

"Everything's fabulous. I have to go. Thanks for the magazines." She didn't smile, she didn't suggest dinner at a later date, and most telling of all, she didn't dig into her candy bag and say, "We love you."

That was my last trip to the house but not the last time I saw her. I ran into Susan and Teri at the mall and the post office. They were perpetually together, indivisible as embryo twins, and never rude, yet I could feel them tugging, eager to shorten our already short exchanges. Once, in the post office lobby, I alluded to the balmy weather and they turned to each other, grinned, and sang in tandem *You Are My Sunshine*, delighting themselves and pushing me, the silent spectator, nearer the foggy perimeter.

"Greg doesn't speak badly of you folks," Frank reported.

"Does he speak of us at all?" I asked.

"No, not really. I said you'd chased a black bear from your yard screaming and banging pots. Nobody said nothing. Oh, Susan did mutter she passed your car on the highway yesterday."

"She waved. That's what she does now. Waves. She used to stop and talk."

The ménage à trois mesmerized Frank. He dropped by their den of sin more often, even though he professed to be sickened by the depravity. Information was scant, but he managed to scrape up fragments. The women thought it was amusing that they were in a race to see who got pregnant first. He learned that prior to marrying Mark, Teri had been vacationing in the mountains, and had met Greg and they had kept in touch. Had they been lovers? Frank hadn't a clue. "Mark's as devastated by Greg's betrayal as he is by Teri's," Frank said. "He figured Greg for a bosom pal." How did Frank know that? He happened to pick up a letter Mark wrote to Teri ("by mistake, without aiming to") when he was alone in their house. What confounded Frank was Teri's knifing her husband in favour of his son. Mark had money; Greg was, by comparison, an impoverished slacker. Money wasn't an issue in the marriage collapse, I said. Mark was controlled by a restless spirit. He would have gotten a house and sired a child or two and then yanked up stakes and ventured elsewhere. It may have been sexual attraction that drew Teri to Greg, but the urge to reside with him was fused with a yearning for permanency, the security of a family unit. Greg, the undisputed monarch of the household, was a father figure to her; Susan a caring sister. Rightly or wrongly, that was how I regarded Teri's defection.

"Doesn't seem like you think those people are busting up any time soon," Frank said.

"Maybe they'll bust up tomorrow, but I'm dubious."

The doubt grew stronger when Teri won the pregnancy race. In Frank's opinion, Susan was practically jumping for joy. She went into Preston and bought a bottle of Seagram's to celebrate. Judith did not jump for joy. She took to her bed the day after Frank relayed the announcement. To combat the public condemnation she despised, she implored Frank to inform everyone in town, i.e., Wally Gossip, that she was disgusted by Greg's decadence and she would never speak to him again. Frank said nothing to anyone. He knew her love for her son would eventually override her abhorrence of community disapproval. Emerging from the bedroom a week or so later, she ordered Frank to drive her to the farm so she could instruct Teri on the dos and don'ts of child-bearing.

As the winter crawled by, Frank's visits to our place dwindled in number. When he did show up, he said he was busy dismantling vehicles at Jablonski's in exchange for a reconditioned Jimmy. He finally admitted that while he really was working at the junkyard it was for a few hours a week — Judith was nagging him to drop us.

"She's got it in her head you folks done something awful to Greg otherwise you'd be buddies."

"We didn't do a blessed thing to Greg," Jessie said.

"I know but I can't budge her. She says I'm disloyal to my family mixing with you two. I'm a grown adult, and I'll go where I please. She hasn't a radar. She can't track me. I'll be damned if I'll stop coming here."

He did, of course. For even if Judith didn't have radar, he must have known he was cheating on her, being disloyal to the family. So now we were friendless. Attempts to change that situation foundered. The town doctor who invited us to his home was fixated on jogging and depressing disease statistics, his wife on clothing and home decor and the square footage of other people's abodes. A farmer we knew foul-mouthed his neighbours, the living and the dead, for two hours. Dinner was distributed from pots set on the table, and when he spilled grape juice on his shirt, the farmer took it off and continued the meal bare-chested. We didn't need friends that badly. In time, we came to believe that the homestead had drawn us so tightly together we weren't missing out on something golden by not socializing with the locals. We felt, curiously enough, like how I thought Greg felt: we were complete, a solid unit, and friends were an accessory we could do quite nicely without.

In the spring, after the May rains, the farmer planning to cultivate our field rode onto the land atop a 1920s classic: a noisy, smoke-exhaling, iron-seated, steel-wheeled Cockshutt. It was illegal to drive a tractor without rubber tires on provincial highways, and he made most of the snail's pace journey from his farm on back roads, towing a flatbed trailer. The boy driving the pickup following the out-dated tractor was about sixteen years of age; the girl seated next to him a year or two younger. The children were the farmer's progeny. His wife was plowing and planting their own fields with a big, smooth-riding, air-conditioned, FM-radio-equipped Aliss-Chalmers. "The wife's darn good at it," he said, paying her a compliment. "She's like a man."

30

Lying fallow for more than a decade, the dirt was firmly compacted and strewn with rocks the earth coughed up, as if choking on them. While his daughter rode the tractor, the farmer and his son loaded the trailer with rocks they piled at treeline. The girl hadn't tilled a field before. "She ain't pretty," her father said, "so she'd better be able to handle machinery if she's counting on marrying a farmer."

The girl wasn't nervous.

I was.

Farm accidents killed and maimed Prairie children by the score. The tractor travelled slowly, halting repeatedly, decreasing the risk of a mishap. Then the rock-picking was over and the harrowing began. The girl, uncaged at last, acted like caution was a distasteful practice. She blasted up and down the field, braking fast and, on the slope, making a sharp turn that, in my inexpert estimation, threatened to pitch the machine sideways. Her father walked onto the field once or twice to offer suggestions, none of which apparently included a reduction in speed, but most of the time he languished in the pickup, smoking cigarettes while his son perused the Boy Scout manual. I was helping Jessie put the garden in, and I glanced at the Cockshutt just as it struck a buried boulder and the girl's body lifted so high off the seat I thought she was heading for the stars.

"I can't stand this," I said to Jessie. "That kid's going to be injured. Did you see her a minute ago? She nearly slammed into a tree."

"It's bothering you, so don't look," Jessie said.

"I can't help it."

"Then go do something else."

"Aren't you worried she'll have an accident?"

"Yes, but her father isn't. He's been farming thirty years and he knows what's safe. He has faith in her. I'm overcoming my reservations and bowing to his judgment."

I hiked up the slope. I slung my recently purchased Golden Hawk chainsaw and a gas can onto the Black Bobcat and drove to the winter wood clearing. Joe had left his Husqvarna behind in case I wanted to get an early start. An early start wasn't my objective. I had my mind set on completing all of the cutting before his arrival at the end of June. It was a mix of self-reliance and the desire to spare Joe's lungs the dangerous intrusion of chainsaw fumes. The Husqvarna had no role in my plot. I had wielded the saw triumphantly in the past, but I remained circumspect. The Golden Hawk was small and lightweight, the blade half the length of the Swedish machine's. It didn't have the power of Joe's saw — in bush speak it was like firing a rabbit-killing .22 instead of a bighorn-bagging .270 Magnum — but poplars weren't as thick as the firs he cut at the Flathead and the American saw readily felled them. I was zipping along, hours into the endeavour, when the Golden Hawk quit flying. It wasn't out of fuel, and the spark plug cap wasn't off. I figured it was overheated, desperate to rest. I figured wrong. After letting it rest for an interval, I was forced to pull the cord almost a dozen times to start the machine, only to have it stop again.

The farmer wheeled his truck up from our field, his son and daughter sitting in the box. The daughter seemed to be unharmed: no gushing blood, no mashed limbs. The farmer said he had an appointment in town and he'd resume working the field first thing tomorrow.

"Madness, sheer madness," he said, vainly trying his hand at awakening the sleeping machine. "A new saw shouldn't act this ornery. It's a lemon. Go to the store and trade it."

"Yes, I suppose I'll have to."

"I didn't know they sold chainsaws this light. My kids could use it. I'll have them help you once you trade saws. It'll be educational. Neither of them has ever touched a chainsaw."

"Thanks for offering," I said, picturing the Honda speeding a disassembled adolescent to the hospital, "but I prefer doing it myself."

The clerk in the Preston store informed me that I had purchased the last Golden Hawk he had in stock. What's more, the saw belonged to a discontinued model line and all sales on discontinued model lines were final, no refunds. He recommended taking it to northern Alberta's lone authorized Golden Hawk dealership repair shop, located in an Edmonton mini-mall. I made the long trip to the city, dropped off the saw, and drove home. When I returned to the shop five days later, the repairman said the machine was in perfect shape; I must have flooded it. He yanked the cord and the engine ignited.

The following morning the Golden Hawk ran for forty-five minutes; then quit and stayed quit. I transported the saw to the porch and, allowing ample time for the flooding to subside, I didn't go near it until dusk. I pulled the cord over and over again and the engine wouldn't fire.

Monday morning, I drove to the repair shop.

When I picked up the saw Friday afternoon, the repairman plunked it on the counter and said accusingly, "Are you cutting trees with this?"

"Yes. Isn't that what chainsaws are for?"

"The Golden Hawk's a suburban saw. You're trimming a lilac bush, you reach for your Golden Hawk. You're shortening a birdhouse pole, you reach for your Golden Hawk. For cutting trees, a heavy-duty saw's necessary. A machine with heft. A Stihl. A Husquvarna."

At the house, I laid the Golden Hawk on the porch next to the firewood box. I'd either concoct a valuable purpose for it by the beginning of next week or I'd heave it in the municipal dump. Monday afternoon, with no valuable purpose in sight, I decided to try and get rid of the saw, which I hated so passionately that I didn't want it anywhere on my land, without travelling all the way to the dump. I went to the highway and placed it on the gravelled shoulder, a thrilling freebie for anyone planning to shorten a bird-house pole. The paucity of traffic was not the significant deterrent to its being claimed that I had anticipated. Nudged by curiosity, I drove to the highway half an hour after I abandoned the Golden Hawk and it was gone.

The success of the roadside disposal experiment precipitated further drop-offs over the years: a boxful of plastic toys and jigsaw puzzles vanished within fifteen minutes; an ironing board took about the same amount of time. The chest of drawers took all afternoon. "The colour stinks," Alex said. "Who wants yellow drawers? Bring it home, paint it white, and put it back on the road tomorrow." After dinner, Jessie and I went to retrieve the chest, not to paint it but to remove it before the black Prairie night covered the highway and a vehicle smashed into it. It was gone. Nothing we placed on the shoulder, in fact, ever failed to capture a new owner. Strangely, in all of the trips I made to check on the status of various objects, I never caught a single person in the act of taking anything. Alex said he knew why I never saw anyone: people weren't taking the stuff, aliens were. They beamed everything up to a space ship. They were eating off our dishes, ironing their clothing on our ironing board and, in a scientific laboratory, conducting tests on his plastic Superman, believing it to be a miniature human in a deep coma.

The illness and the booze were having a softening influence on Joe. Not on his personality, which was unflaggingly bullheaded and inflammable, or on his muscle-lumped limbs, but in the thickening stomach, now smothering his belt, the puffy jowls and the purplish skin drooping under his bloodshot eyes like leaking breast implants. How long would it be before the rest of him turned to seed? He was coughing more frequently, the Prednisone was now accompanied by a prescription painkiller, and he was falling asleep soon after dinner. Yet, Joe being Joe, he said he was disappointed that I had felled the firewood trees. He craved something to do, something manly. I struggled to dream up a time-consuming activity entailing a lean allotment of hard labour, but the only thing I thought of — piling the firewood I split — was brushed aside.

"The river was high this spring," Joe said, swigging beer to help dissolve the pills he had just taken. "It nearly flooded us out."

"Was the restaurant damaged?" Jessie asked.

"The water stopped four feet from the building. A girl's running it while I'm here."

"Floaters?"

"Who?"

"The lady you live with."

"She took off with a logger. Good riddance to bad rubbish. Connie was bone lazy. Cleaning to her was opening the doors and praying a cross-wind blew the dirt outside."

"So you'll be taking Rocky to the Flathead."

"Naw, he's contented here."

"If he's contented, why does he growl at us?"

"He's slow-minded. Give him a spell to get used to you."

"We've had him over two years."

"It won't be much longer. One day you'll wake up with him licking your face. He'll let you stick your arm down his throat and

31

tickle his belly button from the inside and he won't even whimper." He gulped beer, burped, and loosened his belt, as if the last drink added an inch to his waistline. "What's for dinner?"

"For God's sake, dad, it's ten o'clock in the morning. I haven't thought about dinner yet."

"Cabbage rolls would sure hit the spot."

"I don't feel like making cabbage rolls and, if I did feel like it, I haven't a cabbage."

"I'll go to town and buy one."

"Great. Will you make the rolls too?"

"I'm holidaying. I don't cook."

"No cabbage rolls then." Jessie's eyes shifted and pleaded. No words were required but she spoke anyway. "Darling, why don't you show my father the field?"

"I've seen the field," Joe said.

"You haven't seen it with a crop," his daughter countered. "It's not the same."

I showed him the field, the green, low-lying oats aspiring for height and maturity. I told him it was marvellous growing my own goat feed, but the gain wasn't without sacrifice. Uniformity erased the pleasure of surveying an undisciplined spill of weeds and wildflowers and isolated loners, the shrubbery and poplar saplings that detached themselves like runaway children from their bush families. "Why do people poison their lawns with chemicals?" I complained. "Dandelions and buttercups are beautiful. Barren grass isn't."

"You've got that right," Joe said. "Mother Nature knows how things should be. You change them, you're saying she's an idiot."

"You want to walk to the end of the field? The valley looks different from there."

"No, I'm just about ready for another beer." He nodded toward Maya and Bella. They were on the field uprooting plants. "Those clowns will eat the whole crop."

"Not really. We'll be harvesting hundreds of bales."

"When you go for your walks, do the goats follow you?"

"Jessie tethers Maya until I'm up the road. She doesn't have to chain Bella. She won't go anywhere without Maya."

"It must be a nuisance, tethering Maya."

"I'll say. She keeps moving and ducking the chain."

"Fence her in."

"Where, in the garden? She'd be overjoyed."

"We can build a fence around the goat shed. Poplar posts and railings and bush shrubs. A scrap lumber gate. All it will cost you is nails and hinges."

"A fantastic idea," I enthused, even though I thought building the fence would more than likely be a useless effort. Maya was certain to catch on fast that letting Jessie lure her past the gate was submitting to imprisonment, which, no matter how brief, she detested. There wasn't a great deal of difference between attempting to direct her through a gate and chasing her with a tethering chain.

Fortunately for my wife, the nails I had were too small. We had to drive to Preston.

Wally Gossip served us. He had been appointed assistant manager on a permanent basis, and while I couldn't tell if the promotion had swollen his head, it had clearly gone to his company jacket. The pair of ballpoint pens he constantly retained inside the lapel pocket when he was acting assistant manager had been joined by a third ballpoint and a silver-and-blue Waterman.

"So how's the world treating you folks today?" he asked, focusing on Jessie's father, wondering who he was.

"Fairly good," Joe said.

"Glad to hear it. What can I do you for?"

"We don't need help, thank you," I said.

"We're looking for nails," Joe said.

"Nails can be tricky. The wrong length and you've got yourself in a stew. I don't recall us meeting. Are you from Preston?"

"I'm visiting. His wife's my daughter. I'm from the Flathead."

"Where's that?"

"The Rockies."

back
roads
*Ted
Ferguson*

"I've been to the Rockies. Nineteen sixty-eight. Or was it sixty-nine? No, sixty-eight. The year my dad won a prize for his Christmas lights display. Anyhow, I took the Icefields route. The scenery's swell but I didn't dare open the car door. Not in grizzly country."

"Park wardens tell people to lie on the ground and play dead if a grizzly charges them."

"Have you done that?"

"No, sir. Grizzlies stink to high Heaven. A grizzly charges me, I stand still till it's so close the smell's turning my stomach, and then I shoot him dead."

Wally liked to ask questions, Joe liked to answer them. It took an eternity to get the nails. Engrossed with each other, the two men seemed to forget I was with them, which was all right with me, but at the cash register, as the clerk counted my change, Wally did point a question in my direction. "Greg Tyson causing you sleepless nights?"

"Why should he?"

"There's a rumour he's starting a cult. Satan worshippers."

"Ridiculous."

"Could be. Then again, that's how that Hugh Hefner fellow began. Two girls one day, three the next, and before anybody knew it, he had himself a cult. Your wife ought to be careful. Greg'll be smooth-talking her into joining him."

"I don't think Hugh Hefner can be classified as a cult leader," I said.

"Well, I do. What else are all those bunnies at the Playboy Mansion? Slaves to a master. No two ways about it, he's a cult leader."

On our way home, Joe stopped at the mall to buy a cabbage, just in case Jessie changed her mind.

She didn't.

We built the fence. On a test run, Maya eagerly followed Jessie and the apple slices she was holding into the enclosure. The goat gobbled the slices and, to my surprise, lowered herself onto the rough earth, tacitly agreeing to be confined. With the fence erected, Joe was impatient. He missed his café and he missed his

drinking buddies. Scheduled to be with us two weeks, he termi-
nated his stay on the ninth day. He bequeathed the Husqvarna to
me (he owned a newer model) and bluntly stated he wouldn't visit
again unless we had a challenge for him, such as constructing a
guest cabin. It was a proposal he broached each summer, and each
summer we rejected it because it wasn't needed. Jessie promised
to write. She did, occasionally. Her letters were brief and non-
personal, as if she were communicating with someone she met
on a bus tour. The dogs did this, the goats did that, Alex passed
a math exam, we were gaily devouring wild strawberries picked
on Crown land. She didn't have the heart to report that his final
project had been a waste of energy — Maya easily leapt over the
fence the second time Jessie imprisoned her.

When Joe headed to the mountains, I headed to the woodpile. It
felt good to regain control of my days, not having to cope with a
difficult person. The axe rose, the axe fell. The rhythm soothed
and satisfied — until an errant chunk of wood zoomed from the
chopping block and struck my face, cutting my lip and dislodging a front-tooth filling.

My regular dentist in Edmonton had quit the business, which
was a bare-bones way of saying he trashed his office, mailed his
house key to Queen Elizabeth, gave his Cadillac to a doughnut
shop cashier, and rode public transit to a mental institution.

There were two dentists in Preston: Dr. Cruise and Dr. Hyde-
Thornton. Dr. Cruise's reputation was that of a reserved, sensi-
tive person who deemed pulling teeth a horrific event. He was
extremely gentle with needles. Dr. Hyde-Thornton was said to
be a cranky, dandruff-sprinkled Brit who migrated to Canada
because he wasn't efficient enough for the National Health system. He didn't believe in toiling to save decaying teeth; he advocated extraction as a sensible, infallible solution. Presented with
those selections, I booked an appointment with Dr. Cruise.

I was reclining in the padded chair, discussing tartar build-up
with his assistant, when Dr. Cruise entered the room. I recognized

him. He was the out-of-season hunter who almost attacked me when I asked him to leave my land.

"What seems to be the problem?" he asked.

"It isn't serious. I knocked out a filling."

"Let's have a gander."

"I was chopping firewood and a piece flew up and hit me."

He leaned over and examined the tooth.

"What a pity," he said, without a particle of sympathy. "It must have smarted."

The darkness in his speech was twinned with a moonless-night infusion of the eyes. He remembered me and he was sorry a triple root canal wasn't in the cards.

"I'll wear a mouth guard," I said, striving to lighten the atmosphere. "Like a boxer. Like I'm going ten rounds with a cord of poplar."

"Whatever makes you happy," Dr. Cruise said. "There's a speck of decay on the tooth. I won't bother freezing it."

"I prefer the freezing."

"It'll only take a second. You might feel a slight discomfort."

He drilled, and it hurt like hell.

When the filling was securely installed, I beat a path to the door.

"Thank you," I said, God knows why.

"I don't bear grudges," Dr. Cruise said.

"Pardon me?"

"I don't bear grudges."

"Neither do I."

Both of us were lying.

He had hurt me, and rather than face Dr. Cruise's insensitive treatment again, I would seek revenge by depriving him of future dental fees. I would take my business to the competition — the cranky, dandruff-littered tooth-eraser who, a major factor in his favour, tended to use a needle on his patients.

Since the very beginning — that short, exploratory penetration of the bush carrying the faint dream of locating a natural spring — my solitary walks were, as far as distance was concerned, beautifully devoid of pre-established targets. Leaving the house, I never pledged to cover three miles or five or ten on a particular day. I wasn't in training for the Boston Marathon; mileage wasn't an issue. On one occasion, I was only a mile or so east of my quarter, crossing unfamiliar Crown turf, when I came upon a narrow creek dappled by sunlit Douglas fir branches. It was a cool, serene, thoroughly engaging refuge, and although I had anticipated going much farther, I settled on the embankment, took a paperback book from my backpack, and spent several hours beside the creek. Another time, I set out in mid-morning, hiked roughly four miles, and was about to turn back when an antlered moose meandered out of a thicket. He was an ancient specimen, greying and sorrowfully slow, and bald patches blotched his body, possibly the result of rubbing itchy spots against trees. He gazed in my direction without alarm, and it dawned on me that either his vision was shot or he was simply too old to give a damn anymore.

In all of the years I walked through the bush, the only person I encountered was the owner of the pink house. No one hiked the country roads either, but there was the sporadic vehicle and, reasoning that anyone who walked was dirt-poor or in drastic trouble, motorists paused to inquire if I wanted a lift. Greg's Mustang was among the vehicles I came across. It had been two summers since I had last seen the car. Jessie and I had eluded contact with the scandalous trio by travelling to town around noon (Susan and Teri usually went later in the day) and frequenting a different swimming hole. Needless to say, when the Mustang came upon me on the deserted road, Susan, who was alone, didn't brake to ask if I wanted a ride. She iced her face and floored the gas pedal, as though I was the maniacal brute mothers perpetually warned daughters against. Years afterwards, I had my final sighting of the ménage-à-trois women. I was ambling past a vacant clapboard and saw Susan and Teri near the porch, calf-deep in grass and weeds, fussing with Teri's child. Susan was in the mammoth-bellied stage of a pregnancy. Neither woman noticed me. I increased my pace and, beyond the clapboard, plunged into the woods.

There was the odd day, perhaps once a year, when I felt so compelled to walk that I was reluctant to reverse direction. Accumulating an impressive amount of mileage, I spurred myself forward, trusting I would reach a farm where I could phone my wife's Honda-based retrieval service. The outcome of an extended walk on one glorious fall day was a meeting with a local legend. I had descended a timbered slope to an allotment of rolling prairie that, capitulating to nature's rendition of majority rule, soon levelled itself to achieve a state of uninterrupted flatness. I came to a gravel road and a ramshackle farmhouse with peeling paint and a sagging verandah. I knocked, waited, and then cupped my hands to peer through grimy window glass. The parlour was fully furnished. Pictures hugged rose-patterned wallpaper. I proceeded to the rear. In the middle of the yard, Harvey Thomson's scrawny frame stretched on a sun-faded lounge chair. His eyes were shut, his feet were bare, and he was smoking a cigarette. A cocker spaniel slept on the ground near the chair. The townsfolks' claim that Thomson lived in a cave was inaccurate. He lived in a hillside dugout, off to the right of a large, red barn. The dwelling facade blended bottles and mud. There was a window and a door and a tin stove pipe pierced an earthen roof.

"Excuse me — "

"Jesus!" Thomson exclaimed, bounding up.

"I'm sorry. I didn't mean to startle you."

"Why are you sneaking up?"

"I wasn't sneaking up."

"I didn't hear your car. You parked on the road. That's sneaking up."

"I wasn't driving, I was walking. I'd like use your phone, if it's okay with you."

"No phone. Disconnected ages ago."

The cocker spaniel awakened, bolted erect, and heaved itself into a barking fury. A half dozen dogs streaked from the barn. Thomson yelled and raised a hand in the air, calming the running animals. The cocker spaniel fell silent. The other dogs swarmed around me: a border collie licked my hand, a savage-eyed German shepherd sniffed my crotch and mercifully wasn't offended by the smell.

"I have dogs myself," I said.

"What kind?" Thomson asked, suddenly friendlier.

"Black Labs."

"Labs are no dummies. Not like Dalmatians. The IQ of a mosquito. Haven't the common sense to clear out of the way. Fire trucks must flatten them by the hundreds."

Thomson's dogs were, as he put it, cast-offs. City people dumped them in farmers' fields and forested areas. Dogs were discarded for barking. Dogs were discarded for not barking. Dogs were discarded for being sick. Dogs were discarded for being old. Dogs were discarded because their owners scrambled up the social ladder to an elevation where non-purebreds were disdained. Shifts in trends (Shetland sheep dogs hot, Irish wolfhounds cold) wrought dog dumpings. Disconcerting habits — peeing on rugs, drooling, farting, thunderous snoring — were decreed just cause for banishment.

"Why do people drive this far to abandon their pets?" I asked.

"Closer to the city they'd find their way home."

"Then why don't they have them put down?"

"What and feel like murderers?" was Thomson's sarcastic reply. "No can do. Dogs and coyotes are related, you know. Coyotes survive in the wilds, so dogs will adapt jiffy quick. Or a farmer will take them in. Somebody with kids."

Thomson's tender spot for abandoned dogs was as well-known locally as his propensity for barefoot summers and gumboot

back roads
Ted Ferguson

winters. Farmers brought him canines they found. Sometimes Thomson ran an ad in the *Preston Gazette* and readers took dogs off his hands. An equal number of cats were dumped in the countryside, but Thomson spurned them. Cats were creepy and dangerous. He'd heard of a Persian pouncing on a dozing owner and clawing her blind.

"Cats are lazy," I said. "I can't see a cat attacking the person filling its food bowl and letting it nap every five minutes."

"That's your opinion," Thomson said huffily, treating the contradiction like an ankle kick. "Mine is, don't sleep in a room that has a cat in it. You wanted a phone. I'll drive you to my neighbour's. He won't mind you borrowing his."

Thomson dropped me off and I called my wife. Locating me was a cinch. The municipal map in the Honda displayed individual properties and the owners' names. Thomson's neighbour was inquisitive. Did I ever become lost hiking in forests? No, I had a superb sense of direction and a fail-safe back-up system: a pocket compass. I posed a question to him. Why did Thomson renounce shoes and snow boots?

"His answer to that is, 'Use your noggin.' Leastways, that's how he answered me. 'Use your noggin,' he said. 'I am using it,' I said, 'and I can't make rhyme or reason of it.' 'I'm not wasting my breath explaining the obvious,' is what he said. He's a different breed, Harvey Thomson. Not loony like most people say, but different."

"What's wrong with his house? Is it contaminated?"

"Nothing's wrong with his house."

"He doesn't live in it."

"Owing to Betty. She was the love of his life."

"Did she run off with another guy?"

"No, she didn't run off, she died. Betty was his wife. He met her in high school. Harvey and I were pals in those days. I had a girlfriend and the other guys I knew had girlfriends. Everyone had one except Harvey. He was an oddball, and the way of the world is girls won't give oddballs the sweat from their brow unless they're rich. Harvey wasn't rich and he wasn't handsome and we all tagged him for a guy who'd never marry. We were mistaken. In grade twelve, he started dating Betty Nestrenko. To make a long story short, he married her. Betty wasn't what you'd call a looker — a big, plain girl with crooked teeth — but Harvey adored her. About ten years back, Betty got cancer and passed away. Upstairs, in the master bedroom. Harvey couldn't bear going into the house. He was reminded of Betty. So he fixed himself a home in the side of a hill. He goes into the old house now and then to fetch something, but he won't go upstairs, no matter what. People in town look at Harvey's feet and make fun of him. I don't. He's no joke to me; he's a very, very sad individual."

back
roads
*Ted
Ferguson*

33

By the end of April during our first five years in the Dunes, the powers controlling the landscape specified which colour would dominate the coming summer and, uncomprisingly, the colour was a brilliant green. In our sixth year the powers rationed the greenery and imposed a depressingly barren look. I first became alerted to the breach with tradition while walking off our quarter onto the municipal road and casting my eyes to the north. The poplars at the edge of the ravine had shed their leaves. I attributed the shedding to a plant disease that, akin to similar outbreaks I'd observed in the past, was contained in the immediate area. I turned south and dove into the brush without devoting a second thought to the stricken trees.

At dusk the same day, Jessie and I went to sit at the top of the field with pre-dinner glasses of wine. The Crown poplars stationed against the barbed wire at the distant end of the field were stripped naked. The disease was broadening its base, threatening to jump over the fence and infect our trees. The next afternoon, walking onto the municipal road, I looked north and was suddenly distressed. Dozens of trees on our land had turned ugly: most of the leaves were missing, and the trunks and branches were streaked with what appeared to be mounds of dark rot. I walked up the road to estimate how deeply the affliction had spread.

It was then that I realized the streaks were moving.

A disease wasn't denuding the trees, insects were — the obsessive, unbeatable Prairie scourge known as the tent caterpillar.

Within a week the slithery buggers were omnipresent. Eating leaves throughout the Dunes, swarming over Preston and Sunnyside to attack yard and street trees. A Preston radio announcer, comparing the caterpillar hordes to Sherman's liquidating troops, assured listeners, presumably tongue-in-cheek, that the hungry insects were vegetarians and they needn't hide cows, pets, and prepubescent children. *The Noonday Knee-Slapper* aired a joke about a caterpillar and a shoe salesman, and the *Preston Gazette* humorously urged readers to send in recipes for caterpillar casserole.

We weren't laughing at our house.

Thousands of caterpillars swept out of the devastated bush and over the yard. By and large, the goats were unruffled by the invasion. Maya shook her head furiously when an insect crawled past her chin but apart from that she and Bella conducted their daily business as though the insects were too inconsequential to acknowledge. The dogs dealt with the quandary in their own characteristic manner. Drake unhurriedly chewed and spat out caterpillars squirming onto his body while Rocky, in sudden kill-crazy tantrums, rolled in the dirt to squash them. Vowing to preserve the interior of the house as a bug-free refuge, we plucked caterpillars off firewood, clothing and shoes and scanned the dogs before granting them entry.

We expected the caterpillar onslaught to be short-lived. The bugs had, after all, munched practically every leaf on our property, skipping maybe one in three hundred poplars for a reason that baffled us but must have made good sense to a caterpillar. Our expectations were ill-founded. As a massive wave of insects flowed south, plundering Crown trees, thousands arrived in their wake. Frantic for food, the newcomers climbed the house walls and slithered over the roof. The porch steps and landing were blanketed. Jessie swept the insects off the porch with a broom, and the moment they hit the ground Alex walloped them with the flat side of the coal shovel.

One night, at two in the morning, Alex woke up in a panic. He shouted for his mother. Figuring I was an adequate substitute, I leapt from bed and ran upstairs. He had been horrified by a nightmare in which caterpillars crammed his mouth and slid down his throat. I swore that couldn't happen; our vigilance ensured a bugless abode. He fell asleep again. When he awakened at six, there was a caterpillar in his hair. There were more on the staircase and in the living room and kitchen. We tracked and squished them and then sought and pinpointed the access source — bugs were slipping under the building and crawling up an unused heating vent.

The garden was overrun with caterpillars. They weren't eating the plants; they were passing through on a tree quest. Hating the sight of them in our beloved patch, we installed water buckets in the rows and, hand-picking the bugs off plants, Jessie and I drowned them. Alex's method was messier. He accumulated insects in a tomato can, upended the can on a board, and smashed them with a hammer. Whatever system we chose, it was, by virtue of the caterpillars' vast numbers, a David and Goliath confrontation. In the end, negating the hours we dedicated to the ruthless slaughter, Goliath won: the three of us agreed that killing the garden crawlers was a big waste of time.

Nearly three weeks into the invasion, Alex beseeched us to escape to the Dreamland. He hadn't a clue what films were playing, but it was bound to be a double bill. Okay, we said. As long as the stars weren't insects. As long as the movies weren't *The Deadly Mantis* and *Them!* West of Sunnyside, the caterpillar corps grew thinner the further we drove. By the time we rode into Preston the bugs were really scarce. There were a handful in the streets, none outside the Dreamland, and none in the lobby. When a caterpillar climbed the seat in front of me I permitted it to live, figuring it was fated to die soon anyway of abject loneliness. The twin bill opened with a romantic comedy set in Paris (joyously free of insects) and closed with a romantic comedy set in New York (a cockroach in a pantry scene, but compared to the loathsome caterpillars it was charming and cuddly). Previews for a pair of war movies stimulated Alex's imagination. Riding home, he proposed taking a flame-thrower to the caterpillars. If that was a bad idea, how about spraying a couple of barrels of Agent Orange?

The caterpillars may have all but fled Preston, but they weren't ready yet to forsake the Dunes. The morning after the double bill, I peered through kitchen window glass and estimated their numbers to be as enormous as ever. Were they the very same insects — a lost battalion marching in circles, too moronic to fathom the food was gone and to travel elsewhere — or were they recent arrivals belonging to a million-strong army only starting to stream onto our land? I had no way of knowing and no way, without a flame-thrower, of mounting a truly effective counter-attack.

Unwilling to look at more caterpillars than I had to, I suspended my regular walks. Maya, however, was opposed to suspending her daily activity: attempting to crash the forbidden zone. She hawk-eyed the door whenever it was in motion, and inadvertently play-ing the game, I was remiss in fastening the latch one morning as I headed to the garden to water the plants the insects snubbed. Returning to the house, I saw the open door and caterpillars squirming over the threshold. I released a loud curse and, hearing my voice, Bella raced from the kitchen and jumped off the porch landing. Maya was defiant. She reclined on the linoleum floor, chewing the mutilated corpse of the angel hair begonia I had last seen on the counter. I yelled and waved the broom. She scrambled erect and galloped outside. The goats had planted their four-sea-son crop — tiny, round, brown turds — in all of the ground floor rooms. A sugar bowl had been pushed off the table; medicine, perfume, and shampoo bottles littered the bathroom floor; a chair was overturned; a newspaper was torn. Minimal damage. Nothing to be perturbed about if it wasn't for the caterpillars infesting the stove, the furniture, the floors, and the walls.

I summoned my wife. We rounded up the insects, heaped them in jars, and dumped them in the yard. Permitting the cat-erpillars to survive shouldn't be interpreted as a humane gesture. We just didn't want to smear their gooey innards all over the house. We were extremely thorough, removing each piece of fire-wood from the porch box, each piece of chinaware from the cup-boards, and even looking in the ashpan. By noon we thought we had the problem licked, but some caterpillars evaded us. A bug fell into my bath water; another was caught ascending the stair-case. Jessie poured Corn Flakes into a bowl and a caterpillar came out with the cereal. She said she was sick of the bugs and ached to get away. She had the Flathead in mind. One of her father's cabins. We could rent a horse van and take the goats. They could graze the meadow behind the café.

In late afternoon the caterpillar tide receded. The next day it was reduced to a steadily dwindling trickle, sparing us the long trip to the mountains. The insects were cocooning, preparing to partially compensate for the problems they caused us by transforming themselves into gorgeous butterflies.

A local radio report set me straight. Tent caterpillars were not butterfly material. Tent caterpillars hunkered down in their cocoons, and if the eggs they laid survived the winter, their progeny would emerge next spring as ... tent caterpillars.

Awful, bloody awful. A second infestation of hungry bugs; a second summer of inhabiting a scarred landscape. A discouraging prospect, yet not so discouraging that it would send me racing to the city. I was here for the long haul. A caterpillar redux, heavy rains, drought, a cyclone, whatever pain in the butt nature inflicted, I loved the homestead and the valley and I was never going to leave.

It was the summer of 2005, and I was on the elevator of a refurbished Art Deco building in midtown Toronto, whirling up to Alex's third-floor office. Standing behind me, a young woman swathed in black was informing a young man swathed in black that she was spending the Canada Day weekend at her parents' cottage. "I love the country," she said. "The lake's awesome."

"So what do you do with yourself for three days," the man asked, "sit on the dock and throw stones at ducks?"

The woman groaned. "Getouttahere. My parents have a satellite dish and a power boat and there's tons of parties. I come back to the city to catch up on my sleep."

I alighted and sauntered along the marbled corridor. It was my first visit to the building since the company Alex worked for had moved into it. I was early and he was at a staff meeting. I went into his office and sat on his padded chair. E-mail printouts and company brochures lay on the desk, cheek-by-jowl with a computer and laser printer. The desk was strictly business, but the wall-mounted notice board personal. Photographs festooned the cork board: of his wife Kathryn and their young son, of Alex visiting Angkor Wat, of jazz pianist Matthew Shipp, of actress Gloria Graham and, to my surprise, a black and white snapshot of Maya and Bella reclining side by side in the shaded grove between the house and the field.

Alex strode in. "Am I late?"

"No, I'm early."

"What do you feel like eating?"

"How about dim sum? The Rol San."

"Fast, cheap and good. Your favourite things."

The Rol San was bustling. The cashier directed us to a backroom table beneath a framed jigsaw puzzle depicting Charlie Brown and Linus crossing a Hong Kong thoroughfare. We ordered lunch and relaxed in our seats.

E

"I didn't know you had a picture of the goats," I said.

"It's a cool shot. I wish I had more pictures of them."

"I don't recall seeing it before."

"You must have. Mom took it. She sent it to me when I was at Queen's."

That wasn't the only memento she sent him. "Just a little something to remind you of home," she wrote in a note accompanying the goat turd she mailed to Kingston. Alex showed the dropping to his university dorm mates, many of whom were upper-crust snobs whose idea of a pet was their mother's spoiled terrier. A stock broker's son looking forward to a career in drug consumption wondered if he could get high smoking it.

"I dream about the farm sometimes," I said. "Not often, two or three times a year. I miss the summers. The fields and woods and fresh air."

"You're not thinking of moving back?"

"No, I'm here forever."

Isn't that what I said in Alberta — I wasn't ever going to leave?

Well, I meant it when I said it, but circumstances intervened, ushering me in an unexpected direction. And those circumstances didn't include the second caterpillar encroachment, which was as hideous as the first. Mercifully, the third-year attack was minor, a pin prick as opposed to a broadsword slashing. That same year, we added a cat to our household, a pure-white compulsive eater. Lapsang grew fat slaying and digesting mice, rabbits, and birds. His stomach was an inch short of scraping the ground when he walked, but he retained his speed and agility. His appetite was astounding. He feasted on a rabbit, lugged his sagging duffel bag of a belly into the house and, stationing himself by his bowl, pleaded to be fed.

In our tenth year of rural isolation, Lapsang developed a urinary track disease and died. Shortly afterwards, Alex was accepted at Queen's, benefiting from the university's mission to create a balanced social environment by forcing pedigreed youths to associate with people they'd avoid in later life. My wife and

I became casualties of the notorious empty-nest syndrome. We couldn't enter his old room without feeling sad; we peered glumly at passing school buses; we repeatedly discussed the comments he made in long-distance phone calls. Freelance writing was a portable profession (if I could do it in backwoods Alberta I could do it anywhere) but, as strongly as I was tempted to yank up stakes and move to Kingston, I remained committed to the farm. Novelist Margaret Atwood wrote, "A divorce is like an amputation; you survive but there's less of you." Those were my sentiments exactly. Divorced from my son's company, I was a lesser person, an amputee struggling to adjust.

While Alex was in his second year at university, Rocky fell ill. He coughed, he threw up meals, he was lethargic. We took him to the vet. Rocky stiffened and snarled as a clinic helper tried to leash him. Don't worry, the vet told us. I've had cantankerous dogs to contend with. I'll examine him somehow. Go home, I'll phone you tomorrow. The following morning he phoned to say Rocky had bitten his arm. He also said our dog had stomach cancer. With chemotherapy he might live three months. I knew what I had to say but I was unable to say it. Rocky was lovable — in a nutty, snarky, untouchable fashion — and the origin of a hundred family jokes. Like a horse refusing to tread in a frightful place, I balked at being responsible for his death. I told the vet I'd call him back. I drank coffee, I did chores, I stewed. The clinic was closing when I finally phoned and said to forget chemo, put him to sleep.

As anguishing as that was, I faced a worst dilemma months later. Bella fell sick. She stopped eating and lay in the goat shed most of the day. The vet came to the farm. Bella was afflicted with mastitis and should be destroyed while she could still walk and wasn't in constant pain. He examined Maya and pronounced she was in the early stages of the identical ailment. It's best to do it now, he said. It's best to put them both down. My mouth went dry; I was slack-jawed, shaken, and awkward. Realizing the final outcome was inevitable, I didn't ask for time to mull it over. We led the goats deep into the woods and tethered them to trees. The

back roads
Ted Ferguson

vet produced a hypodermic needle and injected Bella's hip. She died instantly, as though an internal light was flicked off. I took an apple from my pocket and handed it to Maya. She was munching enthusiastically as the death drug seized her heart.

The goats were gone.

Rocky was gone.

The cat was gone.

Our son was in the east and proposing to establish his post-university career in Toronto.

The life that used to feel robust and full now seemed shrivelled and depleted.

Two choices loomed, the proverbial crossroads. Acquire more animals and ultimately suffer the agony of having them perish, or decide we were limping towards the end of a natural cycle and the gods were nagging us to pack up and go.

We packed up and went. Joe came from the Flathead to take the propane fridge, the stove, and the Husqvarna. (His breathing had worsened; Jessie and I agreed his days were numbered, but he defied our forecast and lived another ten years). Pastor Bob, a Lutheran minister running a Dunes camp for deaf people, vowed to keep an eye on our land, especially the barbed wire. He had first-hand knowledge of bushland thievery; someone cut the tails off his horses and peddled the hair to an upholstery shop. We sold some things at the Sunnyside auction, loaded the antiques into a moving van, boarded up the empty house, and motored east in the Honda, Drake commanding the back seat. Twelve years in the bush had transformed our perspective. Once scorned and mocked, the city and its cultural and social pleasures now danced in our imaginations like an enchanting seducer, Salome in a concrete Eden.

"Guess who phoned me yesterday," I said as the waiter set a pot of jasmine tea on our table. "Frank Tyson."

"He seems to call you every year."

"Not every year, every two or three years. When Judith forgets he shouldn't be talking to me and orders him to pick up the phone. His son and his women have six kids and Susan's pregnant again. They keep multiplying their clan for the baby bonus cheques. Greg aggravates his father by saying screwing, and not a medical degree, is elevating him to a higher income bracket."

"I wonder how Judith Tyson deals with them having all those babies."

"Frank didn't say, but I'm sure that when she goes to Greg's she acts as though it's perfectly normal, like every man owns and operates two baby factories."

"What else is happening in Preston?"

"There's been some big changes. The drugstore's selling postage stamps and the Preston Hotel's been painted."

"What colour?"

"Off-white."

"I don't remember. What colour was it before?"

"Off-white."

"That can't be the reason he phoned you, to discuss his son and the hotel paint job."

"It wasn't. As usual, he rambled for half an hour and then said Judith was wondering if we were ever coming back, and if we weren't, would we be willing to sell her the land. I said we aren't coming back and we aren't selling. Unless she was willing to pay half a million dollars."

"Half a million? She'd be crazy to pay that. You bought it for twenty-five hundred."

"Who knows. She's determined to have it. Maybe Frank will phone tonight. 'Judith's been saving quarters in peanut butter jars. She's got half a million dollars' worth, and she's shipping them to you next week.'"

"Cool," Alex smiled. "We'll never run out of laundromat coins."

The waiter delivered sticky rice and turnip cakes, and the conversation expanded, flying between books and music, Mario Bava movies and my grandson's fascination with fire engines. We finished lunch and parted on the sidewalk, Alex treading to the salt mines while I headed south on Spadina, launching a lengthy

back roads
Ted Ferguson

[209]

walk in the hot, muggy air. In the years since Jessie and I settled in Toronto the city had lost its sheen (Salome no longer danced), but I enjoyed ambling through the urban melee every afternoon, listening and observing and feeling, paradoxically, both detached and part of a vast machine that was about to jump the rails. Solitude was a condition I was forced to jettison for safety's sake. The week I landed in Toronto, I had gone for a walk in a neighbourhood ravine. There were birds and flowers and lumbering raccoons, and I was alone on the sun-dappled trail, grateful for the silence. Without warning, a filthy giant with lunatic eyes lashed out of underbrush, waving a stick and screeching, "Gimme your doughnuts!" As I didn't have doughnuts, and I didn't anticipate bringing doughnuts in the future, I hurtled past him, automatically deleting walks in secluded places from my daily routine.

Solitude was a sacrifice I regretted, but not all that much. I had something immensely superior: I belonged to a close, caring, fun-to-be-with family. Walking down Spadina, Chinatown retreating from Queen Street's hip, arty glare, I remembered the Vancouver editor shaking his head when I told him I was resigning and going to live in the Alberta bush. "A bad career move," he said. He pegged it accurately; it was a supremely atrocious career move. I made a fair living writing, but I wasn't affluent, I wasn't celebrated, I wasn't Tom Wolfe. Satisfaction is the slipperiest slope to climb in the insanely wired world, and many people I know, the legion of the quietly discontented, neglect their families pursuing job titles and grand homes. The bush years impaired me professionally, but they laid the foundation for what I am today, the rarest of creatures, a twenty-first century man at peace with himself.

Ted Ferguson was born and raised in Victoria, BC. For ten years, he worked as a newspaper reporter, television critic, sports columnist, and magazine writer in several cities across Canada, before becoming a full-time freelance writer 30 years ago. His articles have appeared in the *Globe and Mail*, the *Toronto Star*, *Reader's Digest*, *Canadian Business*, *enRoute*, and the *Imperial Oil Review*. He has published seven books, including the Alberta Non-Fiction Book Award winner, *Desperate Siege*. His last book, *Blue Cuban Nights*, was published in 2002. He currently lives and writes in Toronto.

A Note on the Type
The text is set in
RTF Amethyst. It
was designed by
Canadian printer
Jim Rimmer, who
developed it in
Vancouver from
1994 until 2002.